CONTAGIOUS

CONTAGIOUS

Why Things Catch On

JONAH BERGER

**SIMON &
SCHUSTER**

London · New York · Sydney · Toronto · New Delhi

A CBS COMPANY

First published in Great Britain by Simon & Schuster UK Ltd, 2013
A CBS COMPANY

Photo, p.85: Courtesy of the California Department of Public Health.
Photo, p.88: © 2009 The City of New York, Department of Health and
Mental Hygiene; all rights reserved. Graph, p.91: Based on data provided
by Scott Golder. Photo, p. 96: Gary S. Settles/Photo Researchers, Inc.

1 3 5 7 9 10 8 6 4 2

Simon & Schuster UK Ltd
1st Floor
222 Gray's Inn Road
London WC1X 8HB

www.simonandschuster.co.uk

Simon & Schuster Australia, Sydney
Simon & Schuster India, New Delhi

A CIP catalogue record for this book is available from the British Library

ISBN: 978-1-47111-169-3
ISBN: 978-1-47111-171-6 (ebook)

Printed and bound by CPI Group (UK) Ltd, Croydon, CR0 4YY

To my mother, father, and grandmother.
For always believing in me.

Contents

Introduction: Why Things Catch On   1

Why $100 is a good price for a cheesesteak . . . Why do some things become popular? . . . Which is more important, the message or the messenger? . . . Can you make anything contagious? . . . The case of the viral blender . . . *Six key STEPPS.*

1. Social Currency   29

When a telephone booth is a door . . . Ants can lift fifty times their own weight. . . . Why frequent flier miles are like a video game . . . When it's good to be hard to get . . . Why everyone wants a mix of tripe, heart, and stomach meat . . . The downside of getting paid . . . *We share things that make us look good.*

2. Triggers   61

Which gets more word of mouth, Disney or Cheerios? . . . Why a NASA mission boosted candy sales . . . Could where you vote affect how you vote? . . . Consider the context . . . Explaining Rebecca Black . . . Growing the habitat: Kit Kat and coffee . . . *Top of mind, tip of tongue.*

3. Emotion   93

Why do some things make the Most E-Mailed list? . . . How reading science articles is like standing at the edge of the Grand Canyon . . . Why anger is like humor . . . How breaking guitars can make you famous . . . Getting teary eyed about online search . . . *When we care, we share.*

4. Public   125

Is the Apple logo better upside down than right side up? . . .
Why dying people turn down kidney transplants . . . Using
moustaches to make the private public . . . How to advertise
without an advertising budget . . . Why anti-drug commercials
might increase drug use . . . *Built to show, built to grow.*

5. Practical Value   155

How an eighty-six-year-old made a viral video about
corn . . . Why hikers talk about vacuum cleaners . . . E-mail
forwards are the new barn raising . . . Will people pay to save
money? . . . Why $100 is a magic number . . . When lies spread
faster than the truth . . . *News you can use.*

6. Stories   179

How stories are like Trojan horses . . . Why good customer
service is better than any ad . . . When a streaker crashed the
Olympics . . . Why some story details are unforgettable . . .
Using a panda to make valuable virality . . . *Information travels
under the guise of idle chatter.*

Epilogue   203

Why 80 percent of manicurists in California
are Vietnamese . . . *Applying the STEPPS.*

Acknowledgments   211

Notes   215

Index   235

CONTAGIOUS

Introduction:
Why Things Catch On

By the time Howard Wein moved to Philadelphia in March 2004, he already had lots of experience in the hospitality industry. He had earned an MBA in hotel management, helped Starwood Hotels launch its W brand, and managed billions of dollars in revenue as Starwood's corporate director of food and beverage. But he was done with "big." He yearned for a smaller, more restaurant-focused environment. So he moved to Philly to help design and launch a new luxury boutique steakhouse called Barclay Prime.

The concept was simple. Barclay Prime was going to deliver the best steakhouse experience imaginable. The restaurant is located in the toniest part of downtown Philadelphia, its dimly lit entry paved with marble. Instead of traditional dining chairs, patrons rest on plush sofas clustered around small marble tables. They feast from an extensive raw bar, including East and West Coast oysters and Russian caviar. And the menu offers delicacies like truffle-whipped potatoes and line-caught halibut FedExed overnight directly from Alaska.

But Wein knew that good food and great atmosphere wouldn't be enough. After all, the thing restaurants are best at is going out of business. More than 25 percent fail within twelve months of opening their doors. Sixty percent are gone within the first three years.

Restaurants fail for any number of reasons. Expenses are high—everything from the food on the plates to the labor that goes into preparing and serving it. And the landscape is crowded with competitors. For every new American bistro that pops up in a major city, there are two more right around the corner.

Like most small businesses, restaurants also have a huge awareness problem. Just getting the word out that a new restaurant has opened its doors—much less that it's worth eating at—is an uphill battle. And unlike the large hotel chains Wein had previously worked for, most restaurants don't have the resources to spend on lots of advertising or marketing. They depend on people talking about them to be successful.

Wein knew he needed to generate buzz. Philadelphia already boasted dozens of expensive steakhouses, and Barclay Prime needed to stand out. Wein needed something to cut through the clutter and give people a sense of the uniqueness of the brand. But what? How could he get people talking?

How about a hundred-dollar cheesesteak?

The standard Philly cheesesteak is available for four or five bucks at hundreds of sandwich shops, burger joints, and pizzerias throughout Philadelphia. It's not a difficult recipe. Chop some steak on a griddle, throw it on a hoagie (hero) roll, and melt some Provolone cheese or Cheez Whiz on top. It's delicious regional fast food, but definitely not haute cuisine.

Wein thought he could get some buzz by raising the humble cheesesteak to new culinary heights—and attaching a newsworthy price tag. So he started with a fresh, house-made brioche roll brushed with homemade mustard. He added thinly sliced Kobe beef, marbleized to perfection. Then he included caramelized onions, shaved heirloom tomatoes, and triple-cream Taleggio cheese. All this was topped off with shaved hand-harvested black truffles and butter-poached Maine lobster tail. And just to make it even more outrageous, he served it with a chilled split of Veuve Clicquot champagne.

The response was incredible.

People didn't just try the sandwich, they rushed to tell others. One person suggested that groups get it "as a starter . . . that way you all get the absurd story-telling rights." Another noted that the sandwich was "honestly indescribable. One does not throw all these fine ingredients together and get anything subpar. It was like eating gold." And given the sandwich's price, it was almost as expensive as eating gold, albeit far more delicious.

Wein didn't create just another cheesesteak, he created a conversation piece.

It worked. The story of the hundred-dollar cheesesteak was contagious. Talk to anyone who's been to Barclay Prime. Even if people didn't order the cheesesteak, most will likely mention it. Even people who've never been to the restaurant love to talk about it. It was so newsworthy that *USA Today*, *The Wall Street Journal*, and other media outlets published pieces on the sandwich. The Discovery channel filmed a segment for its *Best Food Ever* show. David Beckham had one when he was in town. David Letterman invited Barclay's executive chef to New York to cook him one on the *Late Show*. All that buzz for what is still, at its heart, just a sandwich.

The buzz helped. Barclay Prime opened nearly a decade ago. Against the odds, the restaurant has not only survived but flourished. It has won various food awards and is listed among the best steakhouses in Philadelphia year after year. But more important, it built a following. Barclay Prime caught on.

WHY DO PRODUCTS, IDEAS, AND BEHAVIORS CATCH ON?

There are lots of examples of things that have caught on. Yellow Livestrong wristbands. Nonfat Greek yogurt. Six Sigma management strategy. Smoking bans. Low-fat diets. Then Atkins, South Beach, and the low-carb craze. The same dynamic happens on a smaller scale at the local level. A certain gym will be the trendy place to go. A new church or synagogue will be in vogue. Everyone will get behind a new school referendum.

These are all examples of social epidemics. Instances where products, ideas, and behaviors diffuse through a population. They start with a small set of individuals or organizations and spread, often from person to person, almost like a virus. Or in the case of the hundred-dollar cheesesteak, an over-the-top, wallet-busting virus.

But while it's easy to find examples of social contagion, it's much harder to actually get something to catch on. Even with all the money poured into marketing and advertising, few products become popular. Most restaurants bomb, most businesses go under, and most social movements fail to gain traction.

Why do some products, ideas, and behaviors succeed when others fail?

One reason some products and ideas become popular is that they are just plain better. We tend to prefer websites that are easier to use, drugs that are more effective, and scientific theories that are true rather than false. So when something comes along that offers better functionality or does a better job, people tend to switch to it. Remember how bulky televisions or computer monitors used to be? They were so heavy and cumbersome that you had to ask a couple of friends (or risk a strained back) to carry one up a flight of stairs. One reason flat screens took off was that they were better. Not only did they offer larger screens, but they weighed less. No wonder they became popular.

Another reason products catch on is attractive pricing. Not surprisingly, most people prefer paying less rather than more. So if two very similar products are competing, the cheaper one often wins out. Or if a company cuts its prices in half, that tends to help sales.

Advertising also plays a role. Consumers need to know about something before they can buy it. So people tend to think that the more they spend on advertising, the more likely something will become popular. Want to get people to eat more vegetables? Spending more on ads should increase the number of people who hear your message and buy broccoli.

But although quality, price, and advertising contribute to products and ideas being successful, they don't explain the whole story.

Take the first names Olivia and Rosalie. Both are great names for girls. Olivia means "olive tree" in Latin and is associated with fruitfulness, beauty, and peace. Rosalie has Latin and French origins and is derived from the word for roses. Both are about the same length, end in vowels, and have handy, cute nick-names. Indeed, thousands of babies are named Olivia or Rosalie each year.

But think for a moment about how many people you know with each name. How many people you've met named Olivia and how many people you've met named Rosalie.

I'll bet you know at least one Olivia, but you probably don't know a Rosalie. In fact, if you do know a Rosalie, I'll bet you know *several* Olivias.

How did I know that? Olivia is a much more popular name. In 2010, for example, there were almost 17,000 Olivias born in the United States but only 492 Rosalies. In fact, while the name Rosalie was somewhat popular in the 1920s, it never reached the stratospheric popularity that Olivia recently achieved.

When trying to explain why Olivia became a more popular name than Rosalie, familiar explanations like quality, price, and advertising get stuck. It's not like one name is really "better" than the other, and both names are free, so there is no difference in price. There is also no advertising campaign to try to get everyone to name their kids Olivia, no company determined to make that name the hottest thing since Pokémon.

The same thing can be said for videos on YouTube. There's no difference in price (all are free to watch), and few videos receive any advertising or marketing push. And although some videos have higher production values, most that go viral are blurred and out of focus, shot by an amateur on an inexpensive camera or cell phone.*

---

* When I use the word "viral" in this book, I mean something that is more likely to spread from one person to another. The analogy to diseases is a good one, but only up to a point. Diseases also spread from person to person, but one key difference is the expected length of the transmission

So if quality, price, and advertising don't explain why one first name becomes more popular than another, or why one YouTube video gets more views, what does?

SOCIAL TRANSMISSION

Social influence and word of mouth. People love to share stories, news, and information with those around them. We tell our friends about great vacation destinations, chat with our neighbors about good deals, and gossip with coworkers about potential layoffs. We write online reviews about movies, share rumors on Facebook, and tweet about recipes we just tried. People share more than 16,000 words per day and every hour there are more than 100 million conversations about brands.

But word of mouth is not just frequent, it's also important. The things others tell us, e-mail us, and text us have a significant impact on what we think, read, buy, and do. We try websites our neighbors recommend, read books our relatives praise, and vote for candidates our friends endorse. Word of mouth is the primary factor behind 20 percent to 50 percent of all purchasing decisions.

Consequently, social influence has a huge impact on whether

---

chain. One person can easily be the initiator of a disease that spreads to a few people, and then from them to a few more people, and so on, until a large number of people have been infected, solely due to that initial individual. Such long chains, however, may be less common with products and ideas (Goel, Watts, and Goldstein 2012). People often share products and ideas with others, but the likelihood that one person generates an extremely long chain may be small. So when I say that doing X will make an idea more viral, for example, I mean that it will be more likely to spread from one person to another, regardless of whether it eventually generates a long chain or "infects" an entire population.

products, ideas, and behaviors catch on. A word-of-mouth conversation by a new customer leads to an almost $200 increase in restaurant sales. A five-star review on Amazon.com leads to approximately twenty more books sold than a one-star review. Doctors are more likely to prescribe a new drug if other doctors they know have prescribed it. People are more likely to quit smoking if their friends quit and get fatter if their friends become obese. In fact, while traditional advertising is still useful, word of mouth from everyday Joes and Janes is at least ten times more effective.

Word of mouth is more effective than traditional advertising for two key reasons. First, it's more persuasive. Advertisements usually tell us how great a product is. You've heard it all—how nine out of ten dentists recommend Crest or how no other detergent will get your clothes as clean as Tide.

But because ads will always argue that their products are the best, they're not really credible. Ever seen a Crest ad say that only one out of ten dentists prefers Crest? Or that four of the other nine think Crest will rot your teeth?

Our friends, however, tend to tell it to us straight. If they thought Crest did a good job, they'll say that. But they'd also tell us if Crest tasted bad or failed to whiten their teeth. Their objectivity, coupled with their candidness, make us much more likely to trust, listen to, and believe our friends.

Second, word of mouth is more targeted. Companies try to advertise in ways that allow them to reach the largest number of interested customers. Take a company that sells skis. Television ads during the nightly news probably wouldn't be very efficient because many of the viewers don't ski. So the company might advertise in a ski magazine, or on the back of lift tickets to a popular slope. But while this would ensure that most people who see the ad like skiing, the company would still end up wasting money because lots of those people don't need new skis.

Word of mouth, on the other hand, is naturally directed toward an interested audience. We don't share a news story or recommendation with everyone we know. Rather, we tend to select particular people who we think would find that given piece of information most relevant. We're not going to tell a friend about a new pair of skis if we know the friend hates skiing. And we're not going to tell a friend who doesn't have kids about the best way to change a diaper. Word of mouth tends to reach people who are actually interested in the thing being discussed. No wonder customers referred by their friends spend more, shop faster, and are more profitable overall.

A particularly nice example of how word of mouth improves targeting came to me in the mail a few years ago. Every so often publishers will send me free books. Usually they're related to marketing and the publisher hopes that if I'm given a free copy, I'll be more likely to assign the book to my students (and sell them a bunch of copies in the process).

But a few years ago, one company did something slightly different. It sent me two copies of the same book.

Now, unless I'm mistaken, there's no reason for me to read the second copy, once I've read the first. But these publishers had a different goal in mind. They sent a note explaining why they thought the book would be good for my students, but they also mentioned that they sent a second copy so that I could pass it along to a colleague who might be interested.

That's how word of mouth helps with targeting. Rather than sending books to everyone, the publishers got me, and others, to do the targeting for them. Just like a searchlight, each recipient of the double mailing would look through his or her personal social network, find the person that the book would be most relevant for, and pass it along.

GENERATING WORD OF MOUTH

But want to know the best thing about word of mouth? It's available to everyone. From Fortune 500 companies trying to increase sales to corner restaurants trying to fill tables. And from non-profits trying to fight obesity to newbie politicians trying to get elected. Word of mouth helps things catch on. Word of mouth even helps B2B companies get new clients from existing ones. And it doesn't require millions of dollars spent on advertising. It just requires getting people to talk.

The challenge, though, is how to do that.

From start-ups to starlets, people have embraced social media as the wave of the future. Facebook, Twitter, YouTube, and other channels are seen as ways to cultivate a following and engage consumers. Brands post ads, aspiring musicians post videos, and small businesses post deals. Companies and organizations have fallen over themselves in their rush to jump on the buzz marketing bandwagon. The logic is straightforward. If they can get people to talk about their idea or share their content, it will spread through social networks like a virus, making their product or idea instantly popular along the way.

But there are two issues with this approach: the focus and the execution.

Help me out with a quick pop quiz. What percent of word of mouth do you think happens online? In other words, what percent of chatter happens over social media, blogs, e-mail, and chat rooms?

If you're like most people you probably guessed something

around 50 or 60 percent. Some people guess upward of 70 percent and some guess much lower, but after having asked this question of hundreds of students and executives, I find that the average is around 50 percent.

And that number makes sense. After all, social media have certainly exploded as of late. Millions of people use these sites every day, and billions of pieces of content get shared every month. These technologies have made it faster and easier to share things quickly with a broad group of people.

But 50 percent is wrong.

Not even close.

The actual number is 7 percent. Not 47 percent, not 27 percent, but 7 percent. Research by the Keller Fay Group finds that only 7 percent of word of mouth happens online.

Most people are extremely surprised when they hear that number. "But that's way too low," they protest. "People spend a huge amount of time online!" And that's true. People do spend a good bit of time online. Close to two hours a day by some estimates. But we forget that people also spend a lot of time offline. More than eight times as much, in fact. And that creates a lot more time for offline conversations.

We also tend to overestimate online word of mouth because it's easier to see. Social media sites provide a handy record of all the clips, comments, and other content we share online. So when we look at it, it seems like a lot. But we don't think as much about all the offline conversations we had over that same time period because we can't easily see them. There is no recording of the chat we had with Susan after lunch or the conversation we had with Tim while waiting for the kids to be done with practice. But while they may not be as easy to see, they still have an important impact on our behavior.

Further, while one might think that online word of mouth reaches more people, that's not always the case. Sure, online conversations *could* reach more people. After all, while face-to-face conversations tend to be one-on-one, or among a small handful of people, the average tweet or Facebook status update is sent to more than one hundred people. But not all of these potential recipients will actually see every message. People are inundated with online content, so they don't have the time to read every tweet, message, or update sent their way. A quick exercise among my students, for example, showed that less than 10 percent of their friends responded to a message they posted. Most Twitter posts reach even fewer. Online conversations *could* reach a much larger audience, but given that offline conversations may be more in-depth, it's unclear that social media is the better way to go.

So the first issue with all the hype around social media is that people tend to ignore the importance of offline word of mouth, even though offline discussions are more prevalent, and potentially even more impactful, than online ones.

The second issue is that Facebook and Twitter are technologies, not strategies. Word-of-mouth marketing is effective only if people actually talk. Public health officials can tweet daily bulletins about safe sex, but if but no one passes them along, the campaign will fail. Just putting up a Facebook page or tweeting doesn't mean anyone will notice or spread the word. Fifty percent of YouTube videos have fewer than five hundred views. Only one-third of 1 percent get more than 1 million.

Harnessing the power of word of mouth, online or offline, requires understanding why people talk and why some things get talked about and shared more than others. The psychology of sharing. The science of social transmission.

The next time you're chatting at a party or grabbing a bite to eat with a coworker, imagine being a fly on the wall, eavesdropping on your conversation. You might end up chatting about a new movie or gossiping about a colleague. You might trade stories about vacation, mention someone's new baby, or complain about the unusually warm weather.

Why? You could have talked about anything. There are millions of different topics, ideas, products, and stories you could have discussed. Why did you talk about those things in particular? Why that specific story, movie, or coworker rather than a different one?

Certain stories are more contagious, and certain rumors are more infectious. Some online content goes viral while other content never gets passed on. Some products get a good deal of word of mouth, while others go unmentioned. Why? What causes certain products, ideas, and behaviors to be talked about more?

That's what this book is about.

One common intuition is that generating word of mouth is all about finding the right people. That certain special individuals are just more influential than others. In *The Tipping Point,* for example, Malcolm Gladwell argues that social epidemics are driven "by the efforts of a handful of exceptional people" whom he calls mavens, connectors, and salesmen. Others suggest that "one in 10 Americans tells the other nine how to vote, where to eat, and what to buy." Marketers spend millions of dollars trying to find these so-called opinion leaders and get them to endorse their products. Political campaigns look for the "influentials" to support their side.

The notion is that anything these special people touch will turn to gold. If they adopt or talk about a product or idea, it will become popular.

But conventional wisdom is wrong. Yes, we all know people who are really persuasive, and yes, some people have more friends than others. But in most cases that doesn't make them any more influential in spreading information or making things go viral.

Further, by focusing so much on the messenger, we've neglected a much more obvious driver of sharing: the message.

To use an analogy, think about jokes. We all have friends who are better joke tellers than we are. Whenever they tell a joke the room bursts out laughing.

But jokes also vary. Some jokes are so funny that it doesn't matter who tells them. Everyone laughs even if the person sharing the joke isn't all that funny. Contagious content is like that—so inherently viral that it spreads regardless of who is doing the talking. Regardless of whether the messengers are really persuasive or not and regardless of whether they have ten friends or ten thousand.

So what about a message makes people want to pass it on?

Not surprisingly, social media "gurus" and word-of-mouth practitioners have made lots of guesses. One prevalent theory is that virality is completely random—that it's impossible to predict whether a given video or piece of content will be highly shared. Other people conjecture based on case studies and anecdotes. Because so many of the most popular YouTube videos are either funny or cute—involving babies or kittens—you commonly hear that humor or cuteness is a key ingredient for virality.

But these "theories" ignore the fact that many funny or cute videos never take off. Sure, some cat clips get millions of views, but those are the outliers, not the norm. Most get less than a few dozen.

You may as well observe that Bill Clinton, Bill Gates, and Bill

Cosby are all famous and conclude that changing your name to Bill is the route to fame and fortune. Although the initial observation is correct, the conclusion is patently ludicrous. By merely looking at a handful of viral hits, people miss the fact that many of those features also exist in content that failed to attract any audience whatsoever. To fully understand what causes people to share things, you have to look at both successes and failures. And whether, more often than not, certain characteristics are linked to success.

ARE SOME THINGS JUST BORN WORD-OF-MOUTH WORTHY?

Now at this point you might be saying to yourself, great, some things are more contagious than others. But is it possible to make anything contagious, or are some things just naturally more infectious?

Smartphones tend to be more exciting than tax returns, talking dogs are more interesting than tort reform, and Hollywood movies are cooler than toasters or blenders.

Are makers of the former just better off than the latter? Are some products and ideas just born contagious while others aren't? Or can any product or idea be engineered to be more infectious?

Tom Dickson was looking for a new job. Born in San Francisco, he was led by his Mormon faith to attend school at Brigham Young University in Salt Lake City, where he graduated in 1971 with a degree in engineering. He moved home after graduation, but the job market was tough and there weren't many opportunities. The only position he could find was at a company making birth control and intrauterine devices. These devices helped prevent pregnancy, but they could also be seen as abortives, which went against Tom's Mormon beliefs. A Mormon helping to develop new methods of birth control? It was time to find something new.

Tom had always been interested in bread making. While practicing his hobby, he noticed that there were no good cheap home grinders with which to make flour. So Tom put his engineering skills to work. After playing around with a ten-dollar vacuum motor, he cobbled together something that milled finer flour at a cheaper price than anything currently on the market.

The grinder was so good that Tom started producing it on a larger scale. The business did reasonably well, and playing around with different methods of processing food got him interested in more general blenders. Soon he moved back to Utah to start his own blender company. In 1995 he produced his first home blender, and in 1999 Blendtec was founded.

But although the product was great, no one really knew about it. Awareness was low. So in 2006, Tom hired George Wright, another BYU alum, as his marketing director. Later, George would joke that the marketing budget at his prior company was greater than all of Blendtec's revenues.

On one of his first days on the job, George noticed a pile of sawdust on the floor of the manufacturing plant. Given that no construction was in progress, George was puzzled. What was going on?

It turned out that Tom was in the factory doing what he did every day: trying to break blenders. To test the durability and power of Blendtec blenders, Tom would cram two-by-two boards, among other objects, into the blenders and turn them on—hence the sawdust.

George had an idea that would make Tom's blender famous.

With a meager fifty-dollar budget (not fifty million or even fifty thousand), George went out and bought marbles, golf balls, and a rake. He also purchased a white lab coat for Tom, just like what a laboratory scientist would wear. Then he put Tom and a blender in front of a camera. George asked Tom to do exactly what he had done with the two-by-twos: see if they would blend.

Imagine taking a handful of marbles and tossing them into your home blender. Not the cheap kind of marbles made of plastic or clay, but the real ones. The half-inch orbs made out of solid glass. So strong that they could withstand a car driving over them.

That is exactly what Tom did. He dropped fifty glass marbles in one of his blenders and hit the button for slow churn. The marbles bounced furiously around the blender, making *rat-tat-tat* noises like a hailstorm on the roof of a car.

Tom waited fifteen seconds and then stopped the blender. He cautiously lifted the top as white smoke poured out: glass dust. All that was left of the marbles was a fine powder that looked like flour. Rather than cracking from the punishment, the blender had flexed its muscles. Golf balls were pulverized, and the rake was reduced to a pile of slivers. George posted the videos on YouTube and crossed his fingers.

His intuition was right. People were amazed. They loved the videos. They were surprised at the blender's power and called it everything from "insanely awesome" to "the ultimate blender." Some couldn't even believe that what they were seeing was possible. Others wondered what else the blender could pulverize. Computer hard drives? A samurai sword?

In the first week the videos racked up 6 million views. Tom and George had hit a viral home run.

Tom went on to blend everything from Bic lighters to Nintendo Wii controllers. He's tried glow sticks, Justin Bieber CDs, and even an iPhone. Not only did Blendtec blenders demolish all these objects, but their video series, titled *Will It Blend?,* received more than 300 million views. Within two years the campaign increased retail blender sales 700 percent. All from videos made for less than a few hundred dollars apiece. And for a product that seemed anything but word-of-mouth worthy. A regular, boring old blender.

The Blendtec story demonstrates one of the key takeaways of contagious content. Virality isn't born, it's made.

And that is good news indeed.

Some people are lucky. Their ideas or initiatives happen to be things that seem to naturally generate lots of excitement and buzz.

But as the Blendtec story shows, even regular everyday products and ideas can generate lots of word-of-mouth if someone figures out the right way to do it. Regardless of how plain or boring a product or idea may seem, there are ways to make it contagious.

So how can we design products, ideas, and behaviors so that people will talk about them?

STUDYING SOCIAL INFLUENCE

My path to studying social epidemics was anything but direct. My parents didn't believe in sweets or television for their children, and instead gave us educational rewards. One holiday season I remember being particularly excited to get a book of logic puzzles, which I explored incessantly over the next few months. These experiences fostered an interest in math and science, and after doing a research project in high school on urban hydrology (how the composition of a stream's watershed affects its shape), I went to college thinking I would become an environmental engineer.

But something funny happened in college. While sitting in one of my "hard" science classes, I started to wonder if I could apply the same toolkit to study complex social phenomena. I had always liked people-watching, and when I did happen to watch TV, I enjoyed it more for the ads than the programs. But I realized that rather than just abstractly musing about why people did things, I could apply the scientific method to find out the answers. The same research tools used in biology and chemistry could be used to understand social influence and interpersonal communication.

So I started taking psychology and sociology courses and got involved in research on how people perceive themselves and others. A few years in, my grandmother sent me a review of a new book she thought I might find interesting. It was called *The Tipping Point.*

I loved the book and read everything related I could find. But I kept being frustrated by a singular issue. The ideas in that book were amazingly powerful, but they were mainly descriptive. Sure some things catch on, but why? What was the underlying human behavior that drove these outcomes? These were interesting questions that needed answers. I decided to start finding them.

After completing my PhD and more than a decade of research, I've discovered some answers. I've spent the last ten years, most recently as a marketing professor at the Wharton School at the

University of Pennsylvania, studying this and related questions. With an incredible array of collaborators I've examined things like

- Why certain *New York Times* articles or YouTube videos go viral
- Why some products get more word of mouth
- Why certain political messages spread
- When and why certain baby names catch on or die out
- When negative publicity increases, versus decreases, sales

We've analyzed hundreds of years of baby names, thousands of *New York Times* articles, and millions of car purchases. We've spent thousands of hours collecting, coding, and analyzing everything from brands and YouTube videos to urban legends, product reviews, and face-to-face conversations. All with the goal of understanding social influence and what drives certain things to become popular.

A few years ago, I started teaching a course at Wharton called "Contagious." The premise was simple. Whether you're in marketing, politics, engineering, or public health, you need to understand how to make your products and ideas catch on. Brand managers want their products to get more buzz. Politicians want their ideas to diffuse throughout the population. Health officials want people to cook rather than eat fast food. Hundreds of undergraduates, MBAs, and executives have taken the class and learned about how social influence drives products, ideas, and behaviors to succeed.

Every so often I'd get e-mails from people who couldn't take the class. They'd heard about it from a friend and liked the material but had a scheduling conflict or didn't find out about it in time. So they asked if there was a book they could read to catch them up on what they missed.

There are certainly some great books out there. *The Tipping Point* is a fantastic read. But while it is filled with entertaining stories, the science has come a long way since it was released over a decade ago. *Made to Stick,* by Chip and Dan Heath, is another favorite of mine (full disclosure: Chip was my mentor in graduate school, so the apple doesn't fall far from the tree). It weaves together clever stories with academic research on cognitive psychology and human memory. But although the Heaths' book focuses on making ideas "stick"—getting people to remember them—it says less about how to make products and ideas *spread,* or getting people to pass them on.

So whenever people asked to read something about what drives word of mouth, I would direct them to the various academic papers I and others had published in the area. Inevitably, some people would e-mail back to say thanks but request something more "accessible." In other words, something that was rigorous but less dry than the typical jargon-laden articles published in academic journals. A book that provided them with research-based principles for understanding what makes things catch on.

This is that book.

SIX PRINCIPLES OF CONTAGIOUSNESS

This book explains what makes content contagious. By "content," I mean stories, news, and information. Products and ideas, messages and videos. Everything from fund-raising at the local public radio station to the safe-sex messages we're trying to teach our kids. By "contagious," I mean likely to spread. To diffuse from person to person via word of mouth and social influence. To be talked about, shared, or imitated by consumers, coworkers, and constituents.

In our research, my collaborators and I noticed some common themes, or attributes, across a range of contagious content. A recipe, if you will, for making products, ideas, and behaviors more likely to become popular.

Take *Will It Blend?* and the hundred-dollar cheesesteak at Barclay Prime. Both stories evoke emotions like surprise or amazement: Who would have thought a blender could tear through an iPhone, or that a cheesesteak would cost anywhere near a hundred dollars? Both stories are also pretty remarkable, so they make the teller look cool for passing them on. And both offer useful information: it's always helpful to know about products that work well or restaurants that have great food.

Just as recipes often call for sugar to make something sweet, we kept finding the same ingredients in ads that went viral, news articles that were shared, or products that received lots of word of mouth.

After analyzing hundreds of contagious messages, products, and ideas, we noticed that the same six "ingredients," or principles, were often at work. Six key STEPPS, as I call them, that cause things to be talked about, shared, and imitated.

Principle 1: Social Currency

How does it make people look to talk about a product or idea? Most people would rather look smart than dumb, rich than poor, and cool than geeky. Just like the clothes we wear and the cars we drive, what we talk about influences how others see us. It's social currency. Knowing about cool things—like a blender that can tear through an iPhone—makes people seem sharp and in the know. So to get people talking we need to craft messages that help them achieve these desired impressions. We need to find our inner remarkability and make people feel like insiders.

We need to leverage game mechanics to give people ways to achieve and provide visible symbols of status that they can show to others.

Principle 2: Triggers

How do we remind people to talk about our products and ideas? Triggers are stimuli that prompt people to think about related things. Peanut butter reminds us of jelly and the word "dog" reminds us of the word "cat." If you live in Philadelphia, seeing a cheesesteak might remind you of the hundred-dollar one at Barclay Prime. People often talk about whatever comes to mind, so the more often people think about a product or idea, the more it will be talked about. We need to design products and ideas that are frequently triggered by the environment and create new triggers by linking our products and ideas to prevalent cues in that environment. Top of mind leads to tip of tongue.

Principle 3: Emotion

When we care, we share. So how can we craft messages and ideas that make people feel something? Naturally contagious content usually evokes some sort of emotion. Blending an iPhone is surprising. A potential tax hike is infuriating. Emotional things often get shared. So rather than harping on function, we need to focus on feelings. But as we'll discuss, some emotions increase sharing, while others actually decrease it. So we need to pick the right emotions to evoke. We need to kindle the fire. Sometimes even negative emotions may be useful.

Principle 4: Public

Can people see when others are using our product or engaging in our desired behavior? The famous phrase "Monkey see, monkey do" captures more than just the human tendency to imitate. It also tells us that it's hard to copy something you can't see. Making things more observable makes them easier to imitate, which makes them more likely to become popular. So we need to make our products and ideas more public. We need to design products and initiatives that advertise themselves and create behavioral residue that sticks around even after people have bought the product or espoused the idea.

Principle 5: Practical Value

How can we craft content that seems useful? People like to help others, so if we can show them how our products or ideas will save time, improve health, or save money, they'll spread the word. But given how inundated people are with information, we need to make our message stand out. We need to understand what makes something seem like a particularly good deal. We need to highlight the incredible value of what we offer—monetarily and otherwise. And we need to package our knowledge and expertise so that people can easily pass it on.

Principle 6: Stories

What broader narrative can we wrap our idea in? People don't just share information, they tell stories. But just like the epic tale of the Trojan Horse, stories are vessels that carry things such as morals and lessons. Information travels under the guise of what seems like idle chatter. So we need to build our own Trojan horses, embedding our products and ideas in stories that people want to tell. But we need to do more than just tell a great story. We need to make virality valuable. We need to make our message so integral to the narrative that people can't tell the story without it.

These are the six principles of contagiousness: products or ideas that contain *Social Currency* and are *Triggered, Emotional, Public, Practically Valuable*, and wrapped into *Stories*. Each chapter focuses on one of these principles. These chapters bring together research and examples to show the science behind each principle and how individuals, companies, and organizations have applied the principles to help their products, ideas, and behaviors catch on.

These principles can be compacted into an acronym. Taken together they spell STEPPS. Think of the principles as the six STEPPS to crafting contagious content. These ingredients lead ideas to get talked about and succeed. People talked about the hundred-dollar cheesesteak at Barclay Prime because it gave them *Social Currency*, was *Triggered* (high frequency of cheesesteaks in Philadelphia), *Emotional* (very surprising), *Practically Valuable* (useful information about high-quality steakhouse), and wrapped in a *Story*. Enhancing these components in messages, products, or ideas will make them more likely to spread and become popular. I hope that ordering the principles this way will make them easier to remember and use.★

★ Note, however, that the recipe analogy breaks down in one respect. The principles are unlike a recipe because not all six ingredients are required to make a product or idea contagious. Sure, the more the better, but it's not as though a product that is Public will fail because it's not wrapped in a Story. So think of these principles less like a recipe and more like tasty salad toppings. Cobb salads, for example, often come with chicken, tomato, bacon, egg, avocado, and cheese. But a salad with just cheese and bacon is still delicious. The principles are relatively independent, so you can pick and choose whichever ones you want to apply.

Some of the principles are easier to apply to certain types of ideas or initiatives. Nonprofits usually have a good sense of how to evoke Emotion,

The book is designed with two (overlapping) audiences in mind. You may have always wondered why people gossip, why online content goes viral, why rumors spread, or why everyone always seems to talk about certain topics around the water cooler. Talking and sharing are some of our most fundamental behaviors. These actions connect us, shape us, and make us human. This book sheds light on the underlying psychological and sociological processes behind the science of social transmission.

This book is also designed for people who want their products, ideas, and behaviors to spread. Across industries, companies big and small want their products to become popular. The neighborhood coffee shop wants more customers, lawyers want more clients, movie theaters want more patrons, and bloggers want more views and shares. Nonprofits, policy makers, scientists, politicians, and many other constituencies also have "products" or ideas that they want to catch on. Museums want more visitors, dog shelters want more adoptions, and conservationists want more people to rally against deforestation.

Whether you're a manager at a big company, a small business owner trying to boost awareness, a politician running for office, or a health official trying to get the word out, this book will help you understand how to make your products and ideas more contagious. It provides a framework and a set of specific, actionable techniques for helping information spread—for engineering stories, messages, advertisements, and information so that people

---

and it's often easier to play up Public visibility for products or behaviors that have a physical component. That said, contagious content often comes from applying principles that originally might have seemed unlikely. Heavy-duty blenders already have Practical Value, but *Will It Blend?* went viral because it found a way to give a blender Social Currency. The video showed how a seemingly regular product was actually quite remarkable.

will share them. Regardless of whether those people have ten friends or ten thousand. And regardless of whether they are talkative and persuasive or quiet and shy.

This book provides cutting-edge science about how word of mouth and social transmission work. And how you can leverage them to make your products and ideas succeed.

1. Social Currency

Among the brownstones and vintage shops on St. Mark's Place near Tompkins Square Park in New York City, you'll notice a small eatery. It's marked by a large red hot-dog-shaped sign with the words "eat me" written in what looks like mustard. Walk down a small flight of stairs and you're in a genuine old hole-in-the-wall hot dog restaurant. The long tables are set with all your favorite condiments, you can play any number of arcade-style video games, and, of course, order off a menu to die for.

Seventeen varieties of hot dogs are offered. Every type of frankfurter you could imagine. The Good Morning is a bacon-wrapped hot dog smothered with melted cheese and topped with a fried egg. The Tsunami has teriyaki, pineapple, and green onions. And purists can order the New Yorker, a classic grilled all-beef frankfurter.

But look beyond the gingham tablecloths and hipsters enjoying their dogs. Notice that vintage wooden phone booth tucked into the corner? The one that looks like something Clark Kent might have dashed into to change into Superman? Go ahead, peek inside.

You'll notice an old-school rotary dial phone hanging on the inside of the booth, the type that has a finger wheel with little holes for you to dial each number. Just for kicks, place your finger in the hole under the number 2 (ABC). Dial clockwise until you reach the finger stop, release the wheel, and hold the receiver to your ear.

To your astonishment, someone answers. "Do you have a reservation?" a voice asks. A reservation?

Yes, a reservation. Of course you don't have one. What would you even need a reservation for? A phone booth in the corner of a hot dog restaurant?

But today is your lucky day, apparently: they can take you. Suddenly, the back of the booth swings open—it's a secret door!—and you are let into a clandestine bar called, of all things, Please Don't Tell.

In 1999, Brian Shebairo and his childhood friend Chris Antista decided to get into the hot dog business. The pair had grown up in New Jersey eating at famous places like Rutt's Hut and Johnny & Hanges and wanted to bring that same hot dog experience to New York City. After two years of R & D, riding their motorcycles up and down the East Coast tasting the best hot dogs, Brian and Chris were ready. On October 6, 2001, they opened Crif Dogs in the East Village. The name coming from the sound that poured out of Brian's mouth one day when he tried to say Chris's name while still munching on a hot dog.

Crif Dogs was a big hit and won the best hot dog award from a variety of publications. But as the years passed, Brian was looking for a new challenge. He wanted to open a bar. Crif Dogs had always had a liquor license but had never taken full advantage of

it. He and Chris had experimented with a frozen margarita ma-
chine, and kept a bottle of Jägermeister in the freezer every once
in a while, but to do it right they really needed more space. Next
door was a struggling bubble tea lounge. Brian's lawyer said that
if they could get the space, the liquor license would transfer. After
three years of consistent prodding, the neighbor finally gave in.

But now came the tough part. New York City is flush with
bars. In a four-block radius around Crif Dogs there are more than
sixty places to grab a drink. A handful are even on the same block.
Originally, Brian had a grungy rock-and-roll bar in mind. But that
wouldn't cut it. The concept needed be something more remarkable. Something that would get people talking and draw them in.

One day Brian ran into a friend who had an antique business.
A big outdoor flea market selling everything from art deco dress-
ers to glass eyes and stuffed cheetahs. The guy said he had found
a neat old 1930s phone booth that he thought would work well
in Brian's bar.

Brian had an idea.

When Brian was a kid, his uncle worked as a carpenter. In
addition to helping to build houses and the usual things that car-
penters do, the uncle built a room in the basement that had secret
doors. The doors weren't even that concealed, just wood that
meshed into other wood, but if you pushed in the right place, you
could get access to a hidden storage space. No secret lair or loot
concealed inside, but cool nonetheless.

Brian decided to turn the phone booth into the door to a secret bar.

Everything about Please Don't Tell suggests that you've been
let into a very special secret. You won't find a sign posted on the

street. You won't find it advertised on billboards or in magazines. And the only entrance is through a semihidden phone booth inside a hot dog diner.

Of course, this makes no sense. Don't marketers preach that blatant advertising and easy access are the cornerstones of a successful business?

Please Don't Tell has never advertised. Yet since opening in 2007 it has been one of the most sought-after drink reservations in New York City. It takes bookings only the day of, and the reservation line opens at 3:00 p.m., sharp. Spots are first-come, first-served. Callers madly hit redial again and again in the hopes of cutting through the busy signals. By 3:30 all spots are booked.

Please Don't Tell doesn't push market. It doesn't try to hustle you in the door or sell you with a flashy website. It's a classic "discovery brand." Jim Meehan, the wizard behind Please Don't Tell's cocktail menu, designed the customer experience with that goal in mind. "The most powerful marketing is personal recommendation," he said. "Nothing is more viral or infectious than one of your friends going to a place and giving it his full recommendation." And what could be more remarkable than watching two people disappear into the back of a phone booth?

In case it's not already clear, here's a little secret about secrets: they tend not to stay secret very long.

Think about the last time someone shared a secret with you. Remember how earnestly she begged you not to tell a soul? And remember what you did next?

Well, if you're like most people, you probably went and told someone else. (Don't be embarrassed, your secret is safe with me.)

As it turns out, if something is supposed to be secret, people might well be *more* likely to talk about it. The reason? Social currency.

People share things that make them look good to others.

MINTING A NEW TYPE OF CURRENCY

Kids love art projects. Whether drawing with crayons, gluing elbow macaroni to sheets of construction paper, or building elaborate sculptures out of recyclables, they revel in the joy of making things. But whatever the type of project, media, or venue, kids all seem to do the same thing once they are finished.

They show someone else.

"Self-sharing" follows us throughout our lives. We tell friends about our new clothing purchases and show family members the op-ed piece we're sending to the local newspaper. This desire to share our thoughts, opinions, and experiences is one reason social media and online social networks have become so popular. People blog about their preferences, post Facebook status updates about what they ate for lunch, and tweet about why they hate the current government. As many observers have commented, today's social-network-addicted people can't seem to stop sharing—what they think, like, and want—with everyone, all the time.

Indeed, research finds that more than 40 percent of what people talk about is their personal experiences or personal relationships. Similarly, around half of tweets are "me" focused, covering what people are doing now or something that has happened to them. Why do people talk so much about their own attitudes and experiences?

It's more than just vanity; we're actually wired to find it pleasurable. Harvard neuroscientists Jason Mitchell and Diana Tamir found that disclosing information about the self is intrinsically rewarding. In one study, Mitchell and Tamir hooked subjects up to brain scanners and asked them to share either their own opinions and attitudes ("I like snowboarding") or the opinions and attitudes of another person ("He likes puppies"). They found that sharing personal opinions activated the same brain circuits that respond to rewards like food and money. So talking about what you did this weekend might feel just as good as taking a delicious bite of double chocolate cake.

In fact, people like sharing their attitudes so much that they are even willing to pay money to do it. In another study, Tamir and Mitchell asked people to complete a number of trials of a basic choice task. Participants could choose either to hang out for a few seconds or answer a question about themselves (such as "How much do you like sandwiches?") and share it with others. Respondents made hundreds of these quick choices. But to make it even more interesting, Tamir and Mitchell varied the amount that people got paid for choosing a particular option. In some trials people could get paid a couple of cents more for choosing to wait for a few seconds. In others they could get paid a couple of cents more for choosing to self-disclose.

The result? People were willing to forgo money to share their opinions. Overall, they were willing to take a 25 percent pay cut to share their thoughts. Compared with doing nothing for five seconds, people valued sharing their opinion at just under a cent. This puts a new spin on an old maxim. Maybe instead of giving people a penny for their thoughts, we should get paid a penny for listening.

It's clear that people like to talk about themselves, but what makes people talk about some of their thoughts and experiences more than others?

Play a game with me for a minute. My colleague Carla drives a minivan. I could tell you many other things about her, but for now, I want to see how much you can deduce based solely on the fact that she drives a minivan. How old is Carla? Is she twenty-two? Thirty-five? Fifty-seven? I know you know very little about her, but try to make an educated guess.

Does she have any kids? If so, do they play sports? Any idea what sports they play?

Once you've made a mental note of your guesses, let's talk about my friend Todd. He's a really cool guy. He also happens to have a Mohawk. Any idea what he's like? How old he is? What type of music he likes? Where he shops?

I've played this game with hundreds of people and the results are always the same. Most people think Carla is somewhere between thirty and forty-five years old. All of them—yes, 100 percent—believe she has kids. Most are convinced those kids play sports, and almost everyone who believes that guesses that soccer is the sport of choice. All that from a minivan.

Now Todd. Most people agree that he's somewhere between fifteen and thirty. The majority guess that he's into some sort of edgy music, whether punk, heavy metal, or rock. And almost everyone thinks he buys vintage clothes or shops at some sort of surf/skate store. All this from a haircut.

Let's be clear. Todd doesn't have to listen to edgy music or shop at Hot Topic. He could be fifty-three years old, listen to Beethoven, and buy his clothes at any other place he wanted. It's not like Gap would bar the door if he tried to buy chinos.

The same thing is true of Carla. She could be a twenty-two-year-old riot grrrl who plays drums and believes kids are for the boring bourgeoisie.

But the point is that we didn't think those things about Carla and Todd. Rather, we all made similar inferences because choices signal identity. Carla drives a minivan, so we assumed she was a soccer mom. Todd has a Mohawk, so we guessed he's a young punk-type guy. We make educated guesses about other people based on the cars they drive, the clothes they wear, and the music they listen to.

What people talk about also affects what others think of them. Telling a funny joke at a party makes people think we're witty. Knowing all the info about last night's big game or celebrity dance-off makes us seem cool or in the know.

So, not surprisingly, people prefer sharing things that make them seem entertaining rather than boring, clever rather than dumb, and hip rather than dull. Consider the flip side. Think about the last time you considered sharing something but didn't. Chances are you didn't talk about it because it would have made you (or someone else) look bad. We talk about how we got a reservation at the hottest restaurant in town and skip the story about how the hotel we chose faced a parking lot. We talk about how the camera we picked was a *Consumer Reports* Best Buy and skip the story about how the laptop we bought ended up being cheaper at another store.

Word of mouth, then, is a prime tool for making a good impression—as potent as that new car or Prada handbag. Think of it as a kind of currency. *Social currency.* Just as people use money to buy products or services, they use social currency to achieve desired positive impressions among their families, friends, and colleagues.

So to get people talking, companies and organizations need to mint social currency. Give people a way to make themselves look good while promoting their products and ideas along the way. There are three ways to do that: (1) find inner remarkability; (2) leverage game mechanics; and (3) make people feel like insiders.

INNER REMARKABILITY

Imagine it's a sweltering day and you and a friend stop by a convenience store to buy some drinks. You're tired of soda but you feel like something with more flavor than just water. Something light and refreshing. As you scan the drink case, a pink lemonade Snapple catches your eye. Perfect. You grab it and take it up to the cash register to pay.

Once outside, you twist the top off and take a long drink. Feeling sufficiently revitalized, you're about to get in your friend's car when you notice something written on the inside of the Snapple cap.

Real Fact # 27: A ball of glass will bounce higher than a ball of rubber.

Wow. Really?

You'd probably be pretty impressed (after all, who even knew glass could bounce), but think for a moment about what you'd do next. What would you do with this newfound tidbit of information? Would you keep it to yourself or would you tell your friend?

In 2002, Marke Rubenstein, executive VP of Snapple's ad agency, was trying to think of new ways to entertain Snapple customers. Snapple was already known for its quirky TV ads featuring the Snapple Lady, a peppy, middle-aged woman with a thick New York accent, who read and answered letters from Snapple fans. She was a real Snapple employee, and the letter writers ranged from people asking for dating advice to people soliciting Snapple to host a soiree at a senior citizens home. The ads were pretty funny, and Snapple was looking for something similarly clever and eccentric.

During a marketing meeting, someone suggested that the space under the cap was unused real estate. Snapple had tried putting jokes under the cap with little success. But the jokes were terrible ("If the #2 pencil is the most popular, why is it still #2?"), so it was hard to tell if it was the strategy or the jokes that were failing. Rubenstein and her team wondered whether real facts might work better. Something "out of the ordinary that [Snapple drinkers] wouldn't know and wouldn't even know they'd want to know."

So Rubenstein and her team came up with a long list of clever trivia facts and began putting them under the caps—visible only after customers have purchased and opened the bottles.

Fact #12, for example, notes that kangaroos can't walk backward. Fact #73 says that the average person spends two weeks over his/her lifetime waiting for traffic lights to change.

These facts are so surprising and entertaining that it's hard not to want to share them with someone else. Two weeks waiting for the light to change? That's unbelievable! How do they even calculate something like that? Think of what else we could do with that time! If you've ever happened to drink a Snapple with a friend, you'll find yourself telling each other which fact you received—similar to what happens when your family breaks open fortune cookies after a meal at a Chinese restaurant.

Snapple facts are so infectious that they've become embedded in popular culture. Hundreds of websites chronicle the various facts. Comedians poke fun at them in their routines. Some of the facts are so unbelievable that people even debate back and forth whether they are actually correct. (Yes, the idea that kangaroos can't walk backward does seem pretty crazy, but it's true.)

Did you know that frowning burns more calories than smiling? That an ant can lift fifty times its own weight? You probably didn't. But people share these and similar Snapple facts because they are *remarkable.* And talking about remarkable things provides social currency.

Remarkable things are defined as unusual, extraordinary, or worthy of notice or attention. Something can be remarkable because it is novel, surprising, extreme, or just plain interesting. But the most important aspect of remarkable things is that they are *worthy of remark.* Worthy of mention. Learning that a ball of glass will bounce higher than a ball of rubber is just so noteworthy that you have to mention it.

Remarkable things provide social currency because they make the people who talk about them seem, well, more remarkable. Some people like to be the life of the party, but no one wants to be the death of it. We all want to be liked. The desire for social approval is a fundamental human motivation. If we tell someone a cool Snapple fact it makes us seem more engaging. If we tell someone about a secret bar hidden inside a hot dog restaurant, it makes us seem cool. Sharing extraordinary, novel, or entertaining stories or ads makes people seem more extraordinary, novel, and entertaining. It makes them more fun to talk to, more likely to get asked to lunch, and more likely to get invited back for a second date.

Not surprisingly, then, remarkable things get brought up more often. In one study, Wharton professor Raghu Iyengar and I analyzed how much word of mouth different companies, products, and brands get online. We examined a huge list of 6,500 products and brands. Everything from big brands like Wells

Fargo and Facebook to small brands like the Village Squire Restaurants and Jack Link's. From every industry you can imagine. Banking and bagel shops to dish soaps and department stores. Then we asked people to score the remarkability of each product or brand and analyzed how these perceptions were correlated with how frequently they were discussed.

The verdict was clear: more remarkable products like Facebook or Hollywood movies were talked about almost twice as often as less remarkable brands like Wells Fargo and Tylenol. Other research finds similar effects. More interesting tweets are shared more, and more interesting or surprising articles are more likely to make the *New York Times* Most E-Mailed list.

Remarkability explains why people share videos of eight-year-old girls flawlessly reciting rap lyrics and why my aunt forwarded me a story about a coyote who was hit by a car, got stuck in the bumper for six hundred miles, and survived. It even explains why doctors talk about some patients more than others. Every time there is a patient in the ER with an unusual story (such as someone swallowing a weird foreign object), everyone in the hospital hears about it. A code pink (baby abduction) makes big news even if it's a false alarm, while a code blue (cardiac arrest) goes largely unmentioned.

Remarkability also shapes how stories evolve over time. A group of psychologists from the University of Illinois recruited pairs of students for what seemed like a study of group planning and performance. Students were told they would get to cook a small meal together and were escorted to a real working kitchen. In front of them were all the ingredients necessary to cook a meal. Piles of leafy green vegetables, fresh chicken, and succulent pink shrimp, all ready to be chopped and thrown into a pan.

But then things got interesting. Hidden among the vegetables and chicken, the researchers had planted a small—but decidedly creepy—family of cockroaches. Eww! The students shrieked and recoiled from the food.

After the bedlam subsided, the experimenter said that some-one must be playing a joke on them and quickly canceled the study. But rather than send people home early, he suggested that they go participate in another study that was (conveniently) taking place just next door.

They all walked over, but along the way they were quizzed about what had happened during the aborted experiment. Half were asked by the experimenter, while the other half were asked by what seemed like another student (who was actually covertly helping the experimenter).

Depending on whom participants happened to tell the story to, it came out differently. If they were talking to another stu-dent—that is, if they were trying to impress and entertain rather than simply report the facts—the cockroaches were larger, more numerous, and the entire experience more disgusting. The students exaggerated the details to make the story more remark-able.

We've all had similar experiences. How big was the trout we caught last time we went fishing in Colorado? How many times did the baby wake up crying during the night?

Often we're not even trying to exaggerate; we just can't recall all the details of the story. Our memories aren't perfect records of what happened. They're more like dinosaur skeletons patched together by archeologists. We have the main chunks, but some of the pieces are missing, so we fill them in as best we can. We make an educated guess.

But in the process, stories often become more extreme or en-tertaining, particularly when people tell them in front of a group.

We don't just guess randomly, we fill in numbers or information to make us look good rather than inept. The fish doubles in size. The baby didn't wake just twice during the night—that wouldn't be remarkable enough—she woke seven times and required skillful parenting each time to soothe her back to sleep.

It's just like a game of telephone. As the story gets transmitted from person to person, some details fall out and others are exaggerated. And it becomes more and more remarkable along the way.

The key to finding inner remarkability is to think about what makes something interesting, surprising, or novel. Can the product do something no one would have thought possible (such as blend golf balls like Blendtec)? Are the consequences of the idea or issue more extreme than people ever could have imagined?

One way to generate surprise is by breaking a pattern people have come to expect. Take low-cost airlines. What do you expect when you fly a low-cost carrier? Small seats, no movies, limited snacks, and a generally no-frills experience. But people who fly JetBlue for the first time often tell others because the experience is remarkably different. You get a large, comfortable seat, a variety of snack choices (from Terra Blues chips to animal crackers), and free DIRECTV programming from your own seat-back television. Similarly, by using Kobe beef and lobster, and charging one hundred dollars, Barclay Prime got buzz by breaking the pattern of what people expected from a cheesesteak.

Mysteries and controversy are also often remarkable. *The Blair Witch Project* is one of the most famous examples of this approach. Released in 1999, the film tells the story of three student filmmakers who hiked into the mountains of Maryland to film a documentary about a local legend called the Blair Witch. They supposedly disappeared, however, and viewers were told that the film was pieced together from "rediscovered" amateur footage that was shot on their hike. No one was sure if this was true.

What do we do when confronted with a controversial mystery like this? Naturally, we ask others to help us sort out the answer. So the film garnered a huge buzz simply from people wondering whether it depicted real events or not. It undermined a fundamental belief (that witches don't exist), so people wanted the answer, and the fact that there was disagreement led to even more discussion. The buzz drove the movie to become a blockbuster. Shot on a handheld camera with a budget of about $35,000, the movie grossed more than $248 million worldwide.

The best thing about remarkability, though, is that it can be applied to anything. You might think that a product, service, or idea would have to be inherently remarkable—that remarkability isn't something you can impose from the outside. New high-tech gadgets or Hollywood movies are naturally more remarkable than, say, customer service guidelines or toasters. What could be remarkable about a toaster?

But it's possible to find the inner remarkability in any product or idea by thinking about what makes that thing stand out. Remember Blendtec, the blender company we talked about in the Introduction? By finding the product's inner remarkability, the company was able to get millions of people to talk about a boring old blender. And they were able to do it with no advertising and a fifty-dollar marketing budget.

Toilet paper? Hardly seems remarkable. But a few years ago I made toilet paper one of the most talked-about conversation topics at a party. How? I put a roll of black toilet paper in the bathroom. Black toilet paper? No one had ever seen black toilet paper before. And that remarkability provoked discussion. Emphasize what's remarkable about a product or idea and people will talk.

LEVERAGE GAME MECHANICS

I was short by 222 miles.

A few years ago I was booking a round-trip flight from the East Coast to California. It was late December, and the end of the year is always slow, so it seemed like a perfect time to visit friends. I went online, scanned a bunch of options, and found a direct flight that was cheaper than the connecting ones. Lucky me! I went to go find my credit card.

But as I entered my frequent flier number, information about my status tier appeared on the screen. I fly a decent amount, and the previous year I had flown enough on United Airlines to achieve Premier status. Calling the perks I was receiving "Premier" seemed like a marketing person's idea of a sick joke, but it was slightly better treatment than you usually get in economy class. I could check bags for free, have access to seats with slightly more leg room, and theoretically get free upgrades to business class (though that never actually seemed to happen). Nothing to write home about, but at least I didn't have to pay to check a bag.

This year had been even busier. I tend to stick with one airline if I can, and in this case, it seemed it might just pay off. I had almost achieved the next status level: Premier Executive.

But the key word here is "almost." I was 222 miles short. Even with the direct flights to California and back, I wouldn't have enough miles to make it to Premier Executive.

The perks for being a Premier Executive were only slightly better than those for Premier. I'd get to check a third bag for free, have access to special airline lounges if I flew internationally, and board the plane seconds earlier than I would have before. Nothing too exciting.

But I was so close! And I had only a few days left to fly the required extra miles. This trip to San Francisco was my last chance.

So I did what people do who are so focused on achieving something that they lose their common sense. I paid more money to book a connecting flight.

Rather than take a direct flight home, I flew a circuitous route, stopping in Boston for two hours just to make sure I had enough miles to make it over the threshold.

The first major frequent flier program was created in 1981 by American Airlines. Originally conceptualized as a method to give special fares to frequent customers, the program soon morphed into the current system of rewards. Today, more than 180 million people accumulate frequent flier miles when they travel. These programs have motivated millions of people to pledge their loyalty to a single airline and stop over in random cities or fly at inopportune times just to ensure that they accrue miles on their desired carrier.

We all know that miles can be redeemed for free travel, hotel stays, and other perks. Still, most people never cash in the miles they accumulate. In fact, less than 10 percent of miles are redeemed every year. Experts estimate that as many as 10 trillion frequent flier miles are sitting in accounts, unused. Enough to travel to the moon and back 19.4 *million* times. That's a lot of miles.

So if they're not actually using them, why are people so passionate about racking up miles?

Because it's a fun game.

_____

Think about your favorite game. It can be a board game, a sport, or even a computer game or an app. Maybe you love solitaire, enjoy playing golf, or go crazy for Sudoku puzzles. Ever stopped to think about why you enjoy these games so much? Why you can't seem to stop playing?

Game mechanics are the elements of a game, application, or program—including rules and feedback loops—that make them fun and compelling. You get points for doing well at solitaire, there are levels of Sudoku puzzles, and golf tournaments have leaderboards. These elements tell players where they stand in the game and how well they are doing. Good game mechanics keep people engaged, motivated, and always wanting more.

One way game mechanics motivate is internally. We all enjoy achieving things. Tangible evidence of our progress, such as solving a tough Solitaire game or advancing to the next level of Sudoku puzzles, makes us feel good. So discrete markers motivate us to work harder, especially when we get close to achieving them. Take the buy-ten-get-one-free coffee punch cards that are sometimes offered at local cafés. By increasing motivation, the cards actually spur people to buy coffee more frequently as they get closer to their tenth cup and claiming their reward.

But game mechanics also motivate us on an *inter*personal level by encouraging social comparison.

A few years ago, students at Harvard University were asked to make a seemingly straightforward choice: which would they prefer, a job where they made $50,000 a year (option A) or one where they made $100,000 a year (option B)?

Seems like a no-brainer, right? Everyone should take option B. But there was one catch. In option A, the students would get paid twice as much as others, who would only get $25,000. In option B, they would get paid half as much as others, who would get $200,000. So option B would make the students more money overall, but they would be doing worse than others around them.

What did the majority of people choose?

Option A. They preferred to do better than others, even if it meant getting *less* for themselves. They chose the option that was worse in absolute terms but better in relative terms.

People don't just care about how they are doing, they care about their performance in relation to others. Getting to board a plane a few minutes early is a nice perk of achieving Premier status. But part of what makes this a nice perk is that you get to board before everyone else. Because levels work on two, well, levels. They tell us where we are at any time in absolute terms. But they also make clear where we stand relative to everyone else.

Just like many other animals, people care about hierarchy. Apes engage in status displays and dogs try to figure out who is the alpha. Humans are no different. We like feeling that we're high status, top dog, or leader of the pack. But status is inherently relational. Being leader of the pack requires a pack, doing better than others.

Game mechanics help generate social currency because doing well makes us look good. People love boasting about the things they've accomplished: their golf handicaps, how many people follow them on Twitter, or their kids' SAT scores. A friend of mine is a Delta Airlines Platinum Medallion member. Every time he flies he finds a way to brag about it on Facebook. Talking about how a guy he saw in the Delta Sky Club lounge is hitting on a waitress. Or mentioning the free upgrade he got to first class. After all, what good is status if no one else knows you have it?

But every time he proudly shares his status, he's also spreading the word about Delta.

And this is how game mechanics boosts word of mouth. People are talking because they want to show off their achievements, but along the way they talk about the brands (Delta or Twitter) or domains (golf or the SAT) where they achieved.

Building a Good Game

Leveraging game mechanics requires quantifying performance. Some domains like golf handicaps and SAT scores have built-in metrics. People can easily see how they are doing and compare themselves with others without needing any help. But if a product or idea doesn't automatically do that, it needs to be "gamified." Metrics need to be created or recorded that let people see where they stand—for example, icons for how much they have contributed to a community message board or different colored tickets for season ticket holders.

Airlines have done this nicely. Frequent flier programs didn't always exist. True, people have flown commercially for more than half a century. But flying was gamified relatively recently, with airlines recording miles flown and awarding status levels. And because this provides social currency, people love to talk about it.

Leveraging game mechanics also involves helping people publicize their achievements. Sure, someone can talk about how well she did, but it's even better if there is a tangible, visible symbol that she can display to others. Foursquare, the location-based social networking website, lets users check in at bars, restaurants, and other locations using their mobile devices. Checking in helps people find their friends, but Foursquare also awards special badges to users based on their check-in history. Check in to the same venue more than anyone else in a sixty-day period and you'll be crowned the mayor of that location. Check in to five different airports and get a Jetsetter badge. Not only are these badges posted on users' Foursquare accounts, but because they provide social currency, users also prominently display them on their Facebook pages.

Just like my Platinum Medallion friend, people display their badges to show off or because they're proud of themselves. But along the way they are also spreading the Foursquare brand.

Great game mechanics can even create achievement out of nothing. Airlines turned loyalty into a status symbol. Foursquare made it a mark of distinction to be a fixture at the corner bar. And by encouraging players to post their achievements on Facebook, online game makers have managed to convince people to proclaim loudly—even boast—that they spend hours playing computer games every day.

Effective status systems are easy to understand, even by people who aren't familiar with the domain. Being the mayor sounds good, but if you asked most people on the street, I bet they couldn't tell you whether that is better or worse than having a School Night badge, a Super User badge, or any one of the more than one hundred other badges Foursquare offers.

Credit card companies struggled with the same issue. Gold cards used to be restricted to people who spent heavily and had a stellar credit history. But as companies started offering them to people with all types of credit, the gold card lost its meaning. So companies came up with new options for their truly wealthy customers: the platinum card, the sapphire card, and the diamond card, among others. But which has more status, a diamond or a sapphire card? Is platinum better or worse than sapphire? This bewildering mix of colors, minerals, and exclusive words creates a chaos of consumer confusion such that people don't know how well they are doing—much less how they compare with anyone else.

Contrast that with medals given out at the Olympics or your local track meet. If entrants tell you they won silver, you know exactly how well they did. Even someone who knows almost nothing about track can tell right away whether an entrant is a star or just doing okay.

Many British supermarkets use a similarly intuitive labeling system. Just as with stoplights, they use red, yellow, or green circles to denote how much sugar, fat, and salt are in different products. Low-sodium sandwiches are marked with a green circle for salt while salty soups get a red circle. Anyone can immediately pick up on the system and understand how to behave as a result.

Many contests also involve game mechanics. Burberry created a website called "Art of the Trench" that is a montage of Burberry and all the people who wear it. Some photos were taken by the world's leading photographers, but people can also send in photos of themselves or their friends wearing the iconic Burberry trench coat. If you're lucky, Burberry posts your image on its website. Your photo then becomes part of a set of images reflecting personal style from across the globe.

Imagine if your photo was picked for the site. What would be your first impulse? You'd tell someone else! And not just one person. Lots of people.

As apparently everyone did. The Burberry site garnered millions of views from more than a hundred different countries. And the contest helped drive sales up 50 percent.

Recipe websites encourage people to post photos of their

finished meals. Weight loss or fitness programs encourage before-and-after photos so people can show others how much better they look. A new bar in D.C. even named a drink, the Kentucky Irby, after my best friend (his last name is Irby). He felt so special he told everyone he knows about the drink and along the way helped spread the word about this new establishment.

Giving awards works on a similar principle. Recipients of awards love boasting about them—it gives them the opportunity to tell others how great they are. But along the way they have to mention who gave them the award.

Word of mouth can also come from the voting process itself. Deciding the winner by popular vote encourages contestants to drum up support. But in telling people to vote for them, contestants also spread awareness about the product, brand, or initiative sponsoring the contest. Instead of marketing itself directly, the company uses the contest to get people who want to win to do the marketing themselves.

And this brings us to the third way to generate social currency: making people feel like insiders.

MAKE PEOPLE FEEL LIKE INSIDERS

In 2005, Ben Fischman became CEO of SmartBargains.com. The discount shopping website sold everything from apparel and bedding to home decor and luggage. The business model was straightforward: companies wanting to offload clearance items or extra merchandise would sell them cheap to SmartBargains, and SmartBargains would pass the deals on to the consumer. There was a broad variety of merchandise, and prices were often up to 75 percent lower than retail.

But by 2007 the website was floundering. Margins had always

been low, but excitement about the brand had dissipated, and momentum was slowing. A number of related websites had also sprung up, and SmartBargains was struggling to differentiate itself from similar competitors.

A year later Fischman started a new website called Rue La La. It carried high-end designer goods but focused on "flash sales" in which the deals were available for only a limited time—twenty-four hours or a couple of days at most. And the site followed the same model as sample sales in the fashion industry. Access was by invitation only. You had to be invited by an existing member.

Sales took off, and the site did extremely well. So well, in fact, that in 2009 Ben sold both websites for $350 million.

Rue La La's success is particularly noteworthy, given one tiny detail.

It sold the same products as SmartBargains. The exact same dresses, skirts, and suits. The same shoes, shirts, and slacks.

So what transformed what could have been a ho-hum website into one people were clamoring to get access to? How come Rue La La was so much more successful?

Because it made people feel like insiders.

When trying to figure out how to save SmartBargains, Fischman noticed that one part of the business was doing incredibly well. Its Smart Shopper loyalty club allowed people who signed up to get reduced shipping fees and access to a private shopping area. Deals that no one else could see. It was a small part of the site, but growth was through the roof.

At the same time, Fischman learned about a concept in France called *vente privée,* or private sale. Online flash sales that were available only for a day. Fischman decided that this was the perfect way to put a unique spin on his business.

And it was. Rue La La hit the ground running because it smartly leveraged the urgency factor. Part of this started by accident. Every morning the site posted new deals at 11:00 a.m. But in the first couple of months demand was so much higher than expected that by 11:03 a.m. everything would be sold out. Gone. So customers learned that if they didn't get there right away, they'd miss out.

As it has grown, Rue La La has maintained this limited availability. It still sells out 40 percent to 50 percent of items in the first hour. Sales have grown, but it's not that revenue gets bigger across the course of the day. The traffic spikes at 11:00 a.m. have simply reached higher and higher levels.

Going to a membership-only model also made the site's members feel like insiders. Just as with the velvet rope that prevents regular partygoers from just walking into an exclusive nightclub, people assumed that if you had to be a member, the site must be really desirable.

Rue La La's members are its best ambassadors. They proselytize better than any ad campaign ever could. As Fischman noted:

> *It's like the concierge at a hotel. You go down to the concierge to find out about a restaurant and he tells you a name right away. The assumption is that he is getting paid to suggest that place and the restaurant is probably mediocre. But if a friend recommends a place you can't wait to get there. Well when a friend tells you you've gotta try Rue La La, you believe them. And you try it.*

Rue La La unleashed the power of friends telling friends.

———

While it might not be obvious right away, Rue La La actually has a lot in common with Please Don't Tell, the secret bar we talked about at the beginning of the chapter. Both used scarcity and exclusivity to make customers feel like insiders.

Scarcity is about how much of something is offered. Scarce things are less available because of high demand, limited production, or restrictions on the time or place you can acquire them. The secret bar Please Don't Tell has only forty-five seats and doesn't allow more people than that in. Rue La La's deals were available for only twenty-four hours; some are even gone within thirty minutes.

Exclusivity is also about availability, but in a different way. Exclusive things are accessible only to people who meet particular criteria. When we think of exclusivity, we tend to think of flashy $20,000 diamond-encrusted Rolexes or hobnobbing in St. Croix with movie stars. But exclusivity isn't just about money or celebrity. It's also about knowledge. Knowing certain information or being connected to people who do. And that is where Please Don't Tell and Rue La La come in. You don't have to be a celebrity to get into Please Don't Tell, but because it is hidden, only certain people know it exists. Money can't buy you access to Rue La La. Access is by invitation only, so you have to know an existing user.

Scarcity and exclusivity help products catch on by making them seem more desirable. If something is difficult to obtain, people assume that it must be worth the effort. If something is unavailable or sold out, people often infer that lots of other people must like it, and so it must be pretty good (something we'll talk more about in the Public chapter). People evaluate cookbooks more favorably when they are in limited supply, find cookies tastier when they are scarce, and perceive pantyhose as higher end when it's less available.

Disney uses this same concept to increase demand for decades-old movies. It takes prime animated features like *Snow White* and *Pinocchio* off the market and puts them in the "Disney Vault" until it decides to reissue them. This limited availability makes us feel like we *have* to act now. If we don't we might miss the opportunity even if we might not have otherwise wanted the opportunity in the first place.★

Scarcity and exclusivity boost word of mouth by making people feel like insiders. If people get something not everyone else has, it makes them feel special, unique, high status. And because of that they'll not only like a product or service more, but tell others about it. Why? Because telling others makes them look good. Having insider knowledge is social currency. When people who waited hours in line finally get that new tech gadget, one of

---

★ Note that making access difficult is different from making it impossible. Sure, getting a reservation at Please Don't Tell is tough, but if people call enough they should be able to snag a reservation. And while Rue La La is open only to members, it recently instituted a policy where even nonmembers can get access by signing up with an e-mail address. Using scarcity and exclusivity early on and then relaxing the restrictions later is a particularly good way to build demand.

Also be wary of how restricting availability can come off as snooty or standoffish. People are used to getting what they want and if they hear "no" too much they may go elsewhere. Jim Meehan at Please Don't Tell addresses this problem explicitly by instructing his staff that if they need to say "no" they should try to figure out a way to say "no, but." Such as, "No, we are all booked up at eight-thirty, unfortunately, but how about eleven?" or "No, we don't have brand X but we have brand Y, would you like to try it?" By managing the disappointment, they maintain the allure while also maintaining customer satisfaction.

the first things they do is show others. Look at *me* and what *I* was able to get!

And lest you think that only exclusive categories like bars and clothes can benefit from making people feel like insiders, let me tell you about how McDonald's created social currency around a mix that includes tripe, heart, and stomach meat.

In 1979, McDonald's introduced Chicken McNuggets. They were a huge hit and every franchise across the country wanted them. But at the time McDonald's didn't have an adequate system to meet the demand. So Executive Chef Rene Arend was tasked with devising another new product to give to the unlucky franchises that couldn't get enough chicken. Something that would keep them happy despite the shortages.

Arend came up with a pork sandwich called the McRib. He had just come back from a trip to Charleston, South Carolina, and was inspired by Southern barbecue. He loved the rich, smoky flavor and thought it would be a perfect addition to the McDonald's menu.

But contrary to what the name suggests, there is actually very little rib meat on the McRib. Instead, imagine a pork patty shaped into something that looks like a rack of ribs. Subtract the bones (and most of the higher-quality meat), add barbecue sauce, top it off with onions and pickles, toss it in a bun, and you pretty much have the McRib.

Lack of rib meat aside, the product test-marketed quite well. McDonald's was excited and soon added the product to the nationwide menu. McRibs were everywhere from Florida to Seattle.

But then the sales numbers came in. Unfortunately, they were much lower than expected. McDonald's tried promotions and features, but not much worked. So after a few years it dropped the McRib, citing Americans' lack of interest in pork.

A decade later, however, McDonald's figured out a clever way to increase demand for the McRib. It didn't spend more money on advertising. It didn't change the price. It didn't even change the ingredients.

It just made the product scarce.

Sometimes it would bring the product back nationally for a limited time; in other cases it would offer it at certain locations but not others. One month it would be offered only at franchises in Kansas City, Atlanta, and Los Angeles. Two months later it would be offered only in Chicago, Dallas, and Tampa.

And its strategy worked. Consumers got excited about the sandwich. Facebook groups started popping up asking the company to "bring back the McRib!" Supporters used Twitter to proclaim their love for the snack ("Lucky me, the McRib is back") and to learn where they could find one ("I only really use Twitter to find out when the McRib is available"). Someone even created an online McRib locator so fans could share locations that offered the sandwich with others. All for what is mostly a mix of tripe, heart, and stomach meat.

Making people feel like insiders can benefit all types of products and ideas. Regardless of whether the product is hip and cool, or a mix of leftover pig parts. The mere fact that something isn't readily available can make people value it more and tell others to capitalize on the social currency of knowing about it or having it.

A BRIEF NOTE ON MOTIVATION

A few years ago I went through a fundamental male rite of passage. I joined a fantasy football league.

Fantasy football has become one of America's most popular unofficial pastimes. For those unfamiliar with the game, it's essentially like being the general manager of an imaginary team. Millions of people spend countless hours scouting players, tweaking their rosters, and watching their performance each week.

It always seemed funny to me that people spent so much time on what is essentially a spectator sport. But when a group of friends needed one more person and asked me if I'd play, I said why not.

And sure enough, I got sucked in. I spent hours every week scanning through cheat sheets, reading up on players I'd never heard of, and trying to find sleepers other people hadn't drafted. Once the season started I found myself watching football, something I had never done before. And it wasn't to see whether my local team won. I was watching teams I knew nothing about, checking out which of my players were doing better, and tweaking my roster each week.

But the most interesting part?

I did this all for free.

No one paid me for the hours I spent, and my friends and I didn't even have a bet riding on the outcome. We were just playing for fun. And, of course, bragging rights. But since doing better than others is social currency, everyone was motivated to do well. Even without a monetary incentive.

The moral? People don't need to be paid to be motivated. Managers often default to monetary incentives when trying to motivate employees. Some gift or other perk to get people to take action. But that's the wrong way to think about it. Lots of people will refer a friend if you pay them a hundred dollars to do so. Offer people the chance to win a gold Lamborghini and they'll do almost anything. But as with many monetary incentives, handing out gold Lamborghinis is costly.

Furthermore, as soon as you pay people for doing something, you crowd out their intrinsic motivation. People are happy to talk about companies and products they like, and millions of people do it for free every day, without prompting. But as soon as you offer to pay people to refer other customers, any interest they had in doing it for free will disappear. Customers' decisions to share or not will no longer be based on how much they like a product or service. Instead, the quality and quantity of buzz will be proportional to the money they receive.

Social incentives, like social currency, are more effective in the long term. Foursquare doesn't pay users to check in to bars, and airlines don't give discounts to frequent flier members. But by harnessing people's desire to look good to others, their customers did these things anyway—and spread word of mouth for free.

PLEASE DON'T TELL? WELL, OKAY.
MAYBE JUST ONE PERSON . . .

How do we get people talking and make our products and ideas catch on? One way is to mint social currency. People like to make a good impression, so we need to make our products a way to achieve that. Like Blendtec's *Will It Blend?* we need to find the inner remarkability. Like Foursquare or airlines with frequent flier tiers, we need to leverage game mechanics. Like Rue La La, we need to use scarcity and exclusivity to make people feel as if they're insiders.

The drive to talk about ourselves brings us back full circle to Please Don't Tell. The proprietors are smart. They understand that secrets boost social currency, but they don't stop there. After you've paid for your drinks, your server hands you a small business card. All black, almost like the calling card of a psychic or wizard. In red script the card simply says "Please Don't Tell" and includes a phone number.

So while everything else suggests the proprietors want to keep the venue under wraps, at the end of the experience they make sure you have their phone number. Just in case you want to share their secret.

2. Triggers

Walt Disney World. Say those words to children under the age of eight and just wait for their excited screams. More than 18 million people from all over the world visit the Orlando, Florida, theme park annually. Older kids love the frightening plummet down Space Mountain and the Tower of Terror. Younger ones savor the magic of Cinderella's castle and the thrill of exploring the rivers of Africa in the Jungle Cruise. Even adults beam joyously when shaking hands with beloved Disney characters like Mickey Mouse and Goofy.

Memories of my own first visit in the early 1990s still make me smile. My cousin and I were picked from the audience to play Gilligan and the Skipper in a reenactment of *Gilligan's Island*. The look of wild triumph on my face when I successfully steered the boat to safety—after being doused with dozens of buckets of water—is still family lore.

Now compare these exhilarating images with a box of Honey Nut Cheerios. Yes, the classic breakfast cereal with a bee mascot that "packs the goodness of Cheerios with the irresistible taste of golden honey." Considered reasonably healthy, Honey Nut

Cheerios is still sugary enough to appeal to children and anyone with a sweet tooth and has become a staple of many American households.

Which of these products—Disney World or Honey Nut Cheerios—do you think gets more word of mouth? The Magic Kingdom? The self-described place where dreams come true?

Or Cheerios? The breakfast cereal made of whole grain oats that can help reduce cholesterol?

Clearly, the answer is Disney World, right? After all, talking about your adventures there is much more interesting than discussing what you ate for breakfast. If word-of-mouth pundits agree on anything, it's that being interesting is essential if you want people to talk. Most buzz marketing books will tell you that. So will social media gurus. "Nobody talks about boring companies, boring products, or boring ads," argues one prominent word-of-mouth advocate.

Unfortunately, he's wrong. And so is everyone else who subscribes to the interest-is-king theory. And lest you think this contradicts what we talked about in the previous chapter about Social Currency, read on. People talk about Cheerios more than Disney World. The reason? *Triggers*.

BUZZING FOR BZZAGENT

No one would mistake Dave Balter for a Madison Avenue shark as portrayed in the popular TV series *Mad Men*. He's young—just forty—and looks even younger, with downy cheeks, wire-rimmed glasses, and a wide-open grin. He's also genuinely passionate about marketing. Yes, *marketing*. To Dave, marketing isn't about trying to convince people to purchase things they don't want or need. Marketing is about tapping into their genuine enthusiasm for products and services that they find useful. Or fun. Or beautiful. Marketing is about spreading the love.

Dave started out as a so-called loyalty marketer figuring out ways to reward customers for sticking with a particular brand. He then created and sold two promotional agencies before founding his current firm, BzzAgent.

Here's how BzzAgent works. Say you're Philips, the maker of the Sonicare electric toothbrush. Sales are good, but the product is new and most people aren't aware of what it is or why they would want to buy one. Existing Sonicare customers are beginning to spread the word, but you want to accelerate things, get more people talking.

That's where BzzAgent comes in.

Over the years, the company has assembled a network of more than 800,000 BzzAgents, people who have said that they are interested in learning about and trying new products. Agents span a broad range of ages, incomes, and occupations. Most are between eighteen and fifty-four years old, are well educated, and have a reasonable income. Teachers, stay-at-home moms, working professionals, PhDs, and even CEOs are BzzAgents.

If you wonder what type of person would be a BzzAgent, the answer is *you*. Agents reflect the U.S. population at large.

When a new client calls, Dave's team culls through its large database to find BzzAgents who fit the desired demographic or psychographic profile. Philips believes its toothbrush will primarily appeal to busy professionals aged twenty-five to thirty-five from the East Coast? No problem, Dave has several thousand on call. You'd prefer working moms who care about dental hygiene? He's got them, too.

BzzAgent then contacts the appropriate agents in its network and invites them to join a campaign. Those who agree get a kit in the mail containing information about the product and coupons or a free trial. Participants in the Sonicare campaign, for example, received a free toothbrush and ten-dollar mail-in rebates for additional toothbrushes to give to others. Participants in a Taco Bell campaign received free taco coupons. Because actual tacos are difficult to send in the mail.

Then, over the next few months, BzzAgents file reports describing the conversations they had about the product. Importantly, BzzAgents are not paid. They're in it for the chance to get free stuff and learn about new products before the rest of their friends and families. And they're never pressured to say anything other than what they honestly believe, whether they like the product or not.

When people first hear about BzzAgent, some argue that it can't possibly work. People don't just spontaneously mention products in everyday conversations, they protest. It just wouldn't seem natural.

But what most people don't realize is that they naturally talk about products, brands, and organizations all the time. Every day, the average American engages in more than sixteen word-of-mouth episodes, separate conversations where they say something positive or negative about an organization, brand, product, or service. We suggest restaurants to coworkers, tell family members about a great sale, and recommend responsible babysitters to neighbors. American consumers mention specific brands more than 3 billion times a day. This kind of social talk is almost like breathing. It's so basic and frequent that we don't even realize we're doing it.

If you want to get a better sense for yourself, try keeping a conversation diary for twenty-four hours. Carry pen and paper with you and write down all the things you mention over the course of a day. You'll be surprised at all the products and ideas you talk about.

Curious about how a BzzCampaign worked, I joined. I'm a big fan of soy milk, so when Silk did a campaign for almond milk, I had to try it. (After all, how can they get milk from an almond?) I used a coupon, got the product from the store, and tried it. It was delicious.

Not only was the product good, it was so good I simply *had* to tell others about it. I mentioned Silk almond milk to friends who don't drink regular milk and gave them coupons to try it themselves. Not because I had to. No one was looking over my shoulder to make sure I talked. I just liked the product and thought others might as well.

And this is exactly why BzzAgent and other word-of-mouth marketing firms are effective. They don't force people to say nice things about products they hate. Nor do they entice people to insert product recommendations artificially into conversations. BzzAgent simply harnesses the fact that people already talk about and share products and services with others. Give people a product they enjoy, and they'll be happy to spread the word.

WHY DO PEOPLE BUZZ ABOUT SOME PRODUCTS MORE THAN OTHERS?

BzzAgent has run hundreds of campaigns for clients as diverse as Ralph Lauren, the March of Dimes, and Holiday Inn Express. Some campaigns were more successful at generating word of mouth than others. Why? Did some products or ideas just get lucky? Or were there some underlying principles driving certain products to get talked about more?

I offered to help find the answer. Enthusiastic at the prospect, Dave gave my colleague Eric Schwartz and me access to data from the hundreds of campaigns he'd run over the years.

We started by testing an intuitive idea: interesting products get talked about more than boring ones. Products can be interesting because they're novel, exciting, or confound expectations in some way. If interest drives talking, then action flicks and Disney World should be talked about more than Cheerios and dish soap.

Intuitively this makes sense. As we discussed in the Social Currency chapter, when we talk to others, we're not only communicating information; we're also saying something about ourselves. When we rave about a new foreign film or express disappointment with the Thai restaurant around the corner, we're demonstrating our cultural and culinary knowledge and taste. Since we want others to think we're interesting, we search for interesting things to tell them. After all, who'd want to invite people to a cocktail party if all they talked about was dish soap and breakfast cereal?

Based on this idea, advertisers often try to create surprising or even shocking ads. Dancing monkeys or ravenous wolves chasing a marching band. Guerrilla and viral marketing campaigns are built on the same notion: Have people dress in chicken suits and hand out fifty-dollar bills on the subway. Do something really different or people won't talk.

But is this actually true? Do things have to be interesting to be discussed?

To find out, we took the hundreds of products that had taken part in BzzCampaigns and asked people how interesting they found each of them. An automatic shower cleaning device? A service that preserves newborn babies' umbilical cords? Both seemed pretty interesting. Mouthwash and trail mix? Not so interesting.

Then we looked at the relationship between a product's

interest score and how frequently it was talked about over the ten-week campaign.

But there was none. Interesting products didn't receive any more word of mouth than boring ones.

Puzzled, we took a step back. Maybe "interest" was the wrong term, potentially too vague or general a concept? So we asked people to score the products on more concrete dimensions, like how novel or surprising they were. An electronic toothbrush was seen as more novel than plastic storage bags; dress shoes designed to be as comfortable as sneakers were seen as more surprising than bath towels.

But there was still no relationship between novelty or surprise scores and overall word of mouth. More novel or surprising products didn't get more buzz.

Maybe it was the people scoring the products. We had first used undergraduate college students, so we recruited a new set of people, of all ages and backgrounds.

Nope. Again the results remained the same. No correlation between levels of interest, novelty, or surprise and the number of times people talked about the products.

We were truly bewildered. What were we doing wrong?

Nothing, as it turned out. We just weren't asking the right questions.

THE DIFFERENCE BETWEEN IMMEDIATE AND ONGOING WORD OF MOUTH

We had been focused on *whether* certain aspects matter—specifically, whether more interesting, novel, or surprising products get talked about more. But as we soon realized, we also should have been examining *when* they matter.

Some word of mouth is immediate, while some is ongoing. Imagine you've just gotten an e-mail about a new recycling initiative. Do you talk about it with your coworkers later that day? Mention it to your spouse that weekend? If so, you're engaging in *immediate word of mouth*. This occurs when you pass on the details of an experience, or share new information you've acquired, soon after it occurs.

Ongoing word of mouth, in contrast, covers the conversations you have in the weeks and months that follow. The movies you saw last month or a vacation you took last year.

Both types of word of mouth are valuable, but certain types are more important for certain products or ideas. Movies depend on immediate word of mouth. Theaters are looking for success right off the bat, so if a film isn't doing well right away, they'll replace it with something else. New food products are under similar pressure. Grocery stores have limited shelf space. If consumers don't immediately start buying a new anticholesterol spread, the store may stop stocking it. In such cases, immediate word of mouth is critical.

For most products or ideas, however, ongoing word of mouth is also important. Antibullying campaigns not only want to get students talking right after the campaign is introduced, they want them to keep spreading the word until bullying is eradicated. New policy initiatives certainly benefit from huge discussion when they are proposed, but to sway voter opinion, people need to keep mentioning them all the way up until Election Day.

But what leads someone to talk about something soon after it occurs? And are these the same things that drive them to keep talking about it for weeks or months after?

To answer these questions, we divided the data on each BzzCampaign into two categories: immediate and ongoing word of mouth. Then we looked at how much of each type of buzz different types of products generated.

As we suspected, interesting products received more immediate word of mouth than boring products. This reinforces what we talked about in the Social Currency chapter: interesting things are entertaining and reflect positively on the person talking about them.

But interesting products did not *sustain* high levels of word-of-mouth activity over time. Interesting products didn't get any more ongoing word of mouth than boring ones.

Imagine I walked into work one day dressed as a pirate. A bright red satin bandana, long black waistcoat, gold earrings, and a patch over one eye. It would be pretty remarkable. People in my office would probably gossip about it all day. ("What in the world is Jonah doing? Casual Friday is supposed to be relaxed, but this is taking it too far!")

But while my pirate getup would get lots of immediate word of mouth, people probably wouldn't keep talking about it every week for the next two months.

So if interest doesn't drive ongoing word of mouth, what does? What keeps people talking?

FROM MARS BARS TO VOTING: HOW TRIGGERS AFFECT BEHAVIOR

At any given moment, some thoughts are more top of mind, or accessible, than others. Right now, for example, you might be thinking about the sentence you are reading or the sandwich you had for lunch.

Some things are chronically accessible. Sports fanatics or foodies will often have those subjects top of mind. They are constantly thinking of their favorite team's latest stats, or about ways to combine ingredients in tasty dishes.

But stimuli in the surrounding environment can also determine which thoughts and ideas are top of mind. If you see a puppy while jogging in the park, you might remember that you've always wanted to adopt a dog. If you smell Chinese food while walking past the corner noodle shop, you might start thinking about what to order for lunch. Or if you hear an advertisement for Coke, you might remember that you ran out of soda last night. Sights, smells, and sounds can *trigger* related thoughts and ideas, making them more top of mind. A hot day might trigger thoughts about climate change. Seeing a sandy beach in a travel magazine might trigger thoughts of Corona beer.

Using a product is a strong trigger. Most people drink milk more often than grape juice, so milk is top of mind more often. But triggers can also be indirect. Seeing a jar of peanut butter not only triggers us to think about peanut butter, it also makes us think about its frequent partner, jelly. Triggers are like little environmental reminders for related concepts and ideas.

Why does it matter if particular thoughts or ideas are top of mind? Because accessible thoughts and ideas lead to *action*.

Back in mid-1997, the candy company Mars noticed an unexpected uptick in sales of its Mars bar. The company was surprised because it hadn't changed its marketing in any way. It wasn't spending additional money on advertising, it hadn't changed its pricing, and it hadn't run any special promotions. Yet sales had gone up. What had happened?

NASA had happened. Specifically, NASA's Pathfinder mission.

The mission was designed to collect samples of atmosphere, climate, and soil from a nearby planet. The undertaking took years of preparation and millions of dollars in funding. When the lander finally touched down on the alien landscape, the entire world was rapt, and all news outlets featured NASA's triumph.

Pathfinder's destination? Mars.

Mars bars are named after the company's founder, Franklin Mars, not the planet. But the media attention the planet received acted as a trigger that reminded people of the candy and increased sales. Perhaps the makers of Sunny Delight should encourage NASA to explore the sun.

Music researchers Adrian North, David Hargreaves, and Jennifer McKendrick examined how triggers might affect supermarket buying behavior more broadly. You know the Muzak you're used to hearing while you shop for groceries? Well, North, Hargreaves, and McKendrick subtly replaced it with music from different countries. Some days they played French music while other days they played German music—what you'd expect to hear outside a French café on the banks of the Seine and what you might expect to hear at Oktoberfest. Then they measured the type of wine people purchased.

When French music was playing, most customers bought French wine. When German music was playing most customers bought German wine. By triggering consumers to think of different countries, the music affected sales. The music made ideas related to those countries more accessible, and those accessible ideas spilled over to affect behavior.

Psychologist Gráinne Fitzsimons and I conducted a related study on how to encourage people to eat more fruits and vegetables. Promoting healthy eating habits is tough. Most people realize they should eat more fruits and vegetables. Most people will even say that they *mean* to eat more fruits and vegetables. But somehow when the time comes to put fruits and vegetables into shopping carts or onto dinner plates, people forget. We thought we'd use triggers to help them remember.

Students were paid twenty dollars to report what they ate every day for breakfast, lunch, and dinner at their nearby dining hall. Monday: a bowl of Frosted Flakes cereal, two helpings of turkey lasagna with a side salad, and a pulled pork sandwich with spinach and fries. Tuesday: yogurt with fruit and walnuts, pepperoni pizza with Sprite, and shrimp pad thai.

Halfway through the two weeks we'd designated for the study, the students were asked to participate in what seemed like an unrelated experiment from a different researcher. They were asked to provide feedback on a public-health slogan targeting college students. Just to be sure they remembered the slogan, they were shown it more than twenty times, printed in different colors and fonts.

One group of students saw the slogan "Live the healthy way, eat five fruits and veggies a day." Another group saw "Each and every dining-hall tray needs five fruits and veggies a day." Both slogans encouraged people to eat fruits and vegetables, but the tray slogan did so using a trigger. The students lived on campus, and many of them ate in dining halls that used trays. So we wanted to see if we could trigger healthy eating behavior by using the dining room tray to remind students of the slogan.

Our students didn't care for the tray slogan. They called it "corny" and rated it as less than half as attractive as the more generic "live healthy" slogan. Further, when asked whether the slogan would influence their own fruit and vegetable consumption, the students who had been shown the "tray" slogan were significantly more likely to say no.

But when it came to actual behavior, the effects were striking. Students who had been shown the more generic "live healthy" slogan didn't change their eating habits. But students who had seen the "tray" slogan and used trays in their cafeterias markedly changed their behavior. The trays reminded them of the slogan and they ate 25 percent more fruits and vegetables as a result. The trigger worked.

We were pretty excited by the results. Getting college students to do anything—let alone eat more fruits and vegetables—is an impressive feat.

But when a colleague of ours heard about the study he wondered whether triggers would impact an even more consequential behavior: voting.

Where did you cast your ballot in the last election?

Most people will answer this question with the name of their city or state. Evanston. Birmingham. Florida. Nevada. If asked to clarify, they might add "near my office" or "across from the supermarket." Few will be more specific. And why should they be? Although geography clearly matters in voting—the East Coast leans Democratic while the South skews Republican—few people would think that the exact venue in which they vote matters.

But it does.

Political scientists usually assume that voting is based on rational and stable preferences: people possess core beliefs and weigh costs and benefits when deciding how to vote. If we care about the environment, we vote for candidates who promise to protect natural resources. If we're concerned about health care, we support initiatives to make it more affordable and available to greater numbers of people. In this calculating, cognitive model of voting behavior, the particular kind of building people happen to cast their ballot in shouldn't affect behavior.

But in light of what we were learning about triggers, we weren't so sure. Most people in the United States are assigned to vote at a particular polling location. They are typically public buildings—firehouses, courthouses, or schools—but can also be churches, private office buildings, or other venues.

Different locations contain different triggers. Churches are filled with religious imagery, which might remind people of church doctrine. Schools are filled with lockers, desks, and chalkboards, which might remind people of children or early educational experiences. And once these thoughts are triggered, they might change behavior.

Could voting in a church lead people to think more negatively about abortion or gay marriage? Could voting in a school lead people to support education funding?

To test this idea, Marc Meredith, Christian Wheeler, and I acquired data from each polling place in Arizona's 2000 general election. We used the name and address of each polling location to determine whether it was a church, a school, or some other type of building. Forty percent of people were assigned to vote in churches, 26 percent in schools, 10 percent in community centers, and the rest in a mix of apartment buildings, golf courses, and even RV parks.

Then we examined whether people voted differently at different types of polling places. In particular, we focused on a ballot initiative that proposed raising the sales tax from 5.0 percent to 5.6 percent to support public schools. This initiative had been hotly debated, with good arguments on both sides. Most people support education but few people enjoy paying more taxes. It was a tough decision.

If where people voted didn't matter, then the percent supporting the initiative should be the same at schools and other polling locations.

But it wasn't. More than ten thousand more people voted in favor of the school funding initiative when the polling place was a school. Polling location had a dramatic impact on voting behavior.

And the initiative passed.

This difference persisted even after we controlled for things like regional differences in political preferences and demographics. We even compared two similar groups of voters to double-check our findings. People who lived near schools and were assigned to vote at one versus people who lived near schools but were assigned to vote at a different type of polling place (such as a firehouse). A significantly higher percentage of the people who voted in schools were in favor of increasing funding for schools. The fact that they were *in* a school when they voted triggered more school-friendly behavior.

A ten-thousand-vote difference in a statewide election might not seem like much. But it was more than enough to shift a close election. In the 2000 presidential election the difference between George Bush and Al Gore came down to less than 1,000 votes. If 1,000 votes is enough to shift an election, 10,000 certainly could. Triggers matter.

So how do triggers help determine whether products and ideas catch on?

SEARCHING FOR "FRIDAY" ON . . . FRIDAY

In 2011, Rebecca Black accomplished a momentous achievement. The thirteen-year-old released what many music critics dubbed the worst song ever.

Born in 1997, Rebecca was just a kid when she released her first full-length song. But this was far from her first foray into music. She had auditioned for shows, had attended music summer camp, and had sung publicly for a number of years. After hearing from a classmate who had turned to outside help for her music career, Rebecca's parents paid four thousand dollars to ARK Music Factory, a Los Angeles label, to write a song for their daughter to sing.

The result was decidedly, well, awful. Entitled "Friday," the tune was a whiny, overproduced number about teenage life and the joys of the weekend. The song starts with her getting up in the morning and getting ready to go to school:

Seven a.m., waking up in the morning
Gotta be fresh, gotta go downstairs
Gotta have my bowl, gotta have cereal

Then she hustles down to the bus stop, sees her friends drive by, and ponders whether to sit in the front seat or the back. Finally, after all those tough decisions, she hits the chorus, an ode to her excitement about the impending two days of freedom:

It's Friday, Friday
Gotta get down on Friday
Everybody's lookin' forward to the weekend, weekend.

All in all, the piece sounds more like a monologue of the random thoughts going through an especially vacant teenager's head than a real song.

Yet this song was one of the most viral videos of 2011. It was viewed more than 300 million times on YouTube, and many millions more listened to it over other channels.

Why? The song was terrible, but lots of songs are terrible. So what made this one a success?

Take a look at the number of daily searches for "Rebecca Black" on YouTube in March 2011, soon after the song was first released. See if you notice a pattern.

Searches for "Rebecca Black" on YouTube

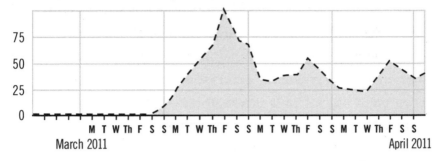

Notice the spike once every week? Look closer and you'll see that the spike happens on the same day every week. There was one on March 18, seven days later on March 25, and seven days later, on April 1.

The particular day of the week? You guessed it. Friday—just like the name of Rebecca Black's song.

So while the song was equally bad every day of the week, each Friday it received a strong trigger that contributed to its success.

TRIGGERED TO TALK

As discussed in the Social Currency chapter, some word of mouth is motivated by peoples' desire to look good to others. Mentioning clever or entertaining things makes people seem clever and entertaining. But that isn't the only factor that drives us to share.

Most conversations can be described as small talk. We chat with parents at our kids' soccer games or schmooze with coworkers in the break room. These conversations are less about finding interesting things to say to make us look good than they are about filling conversational space. We don't want to sit there silently, so we talk about something. Anything. Our goal isn't necessarily to prove that we are interesting, funny, or intelligent. We just want to say something to keep the conversation going. Anything to prove that we're not terrible conversationalists.

So what do we talk about? Whatever is top of mind is a good place to start. If something is accessible, it's usually relevant to the situation at hand. Did you read about the new bridge construction? What did you think about the game last night?

We talk about these topics because they are going on in the surrounding environment. We saw the bulldozers on our drive in, so construction is on our mind. We bump into a friend who likes sports, so we think about the big game. Triggers boost word of mouth.

Returning to the BzzAgent data, triggers helped us answer why some products get talked about more. More frequently triggered products got 15 percent more word of mouth. Even mundane products like Ziploc bags and moisturizer received lots of buzz because people were triggered to think about them so frequently. People who use moisturizer often apply it at least once a day. People often use Ziploc bags after meals to wrap up leftovers. These everyday activities make those products more top of mind and, as a result, lead them to be talked about more.

Furthermore, not only did triggered products get more immediate word of mouth, they also got more word of mouth on an ongoing basis.

In this way, Ziploc bags are the antithesis of me going to

teach dressed like a pirate. The pirate story is interesting, but it's here today, gone tomorrow. Ziploc bags may be boring, but they get mentioned week in and week out because they are frequently triggered. By acting as reminders, triggers not only get people talking, they keep them talking. Top of mind means tip of tongue.

So rather than just going for a catchy message, consider the context. Think about whether the message will be triggered by the everyday environments of the target audience. Going for interesting is our default tendency. Whether running for class president or selling soda, we think that catchy or clever slogans will get us where we need to go.

But as we saw in our fruits and vegetables study, a strong trigger can be much more effective than a catchy slogan. Even though they hated the slogan, college students ate more fruits and vegetables when cafeteria trays triggered reminders of the health benefits. Just being exposed to a clever slogan didn't change behavior at all.

A few years ago, auto insurance company GEICO ran ads that said switching to GEICO was so simple that even a caveman could do it. On the cleverness dimension the ads were great. They were funny and made the point that switching to GEICO was easy.

But judged on triggers, the ads fail. We don't see many cavemen in our daily lives, so the ad is unlikely to come to mind often, making it less likely to be talked about.

Contrast that with the Budweiser beer "Wassup?" campaign. Two guys are talking on the phone while drinking Budweiser and watching a basketball game on television. A third friend arrives. He yells, "Wassup?" One of the first two guys yells

"Wassup?" back. This kicks off an endless cycle of wassups between a growing number of Budweiser-drinking buddies.

No, it wasn't the cleverest of commercials. But it became
a global phenomenon. And at least part of its success was due
to triggers. Budweiser considered the context. "Wassup" was a
popular greeting among young men at the time. Just greeting
friends triggered thoughts of Budweiser in Budweiser's prime
demographic.

The more the desired behavior happens after a delay, the
more important being triggered becomes. Market research
often focuses on consumers' immediate reaction to an advertising message or campaign. That might be valuable in situations
where the consumer is immediately offered a chance to buy the
product. But in most cases, people hear an ad one day and then
go to the store days or weeks later. If they're not triggered to
think about it, how will they remember that ad when they're at
the store?

Public health campaigns would also benefit from considering the context. Take messages that encourage college students
to drink responsibly. While the messages might be really clever
and convincing, they're posted at the campus health center, far
away from the frat houses or other places where students actually
drink. So while students may agree with the message when they
read it, unless they are triggered to think about it when they are
actually drinking, the message is unlikely to change behavior.

Triggers even shed light on when negative word of mouth
has positive effects. Economist Alan Sorensen, Scott Rasmussen,
and I analyzed hundreds of *New York Times* book reviews to see
how positive and negative reviews affected book sales.

In contrast to the notion that any publicity is good publicity,
negative reviews hurt sales for some books. But for books by new

or relatively unknown authors, negative reviews increased sales by 45 percent. A book called *Fierce People,* for example, got a terrible review. The *Times* noted that the author "does not have a particularly sharp eye" and complained that "the change in tone is so abrupt that the dissonance it creates is almost distasteful." Yet sales more than quadrupled after the review.

Triggers explain why. Even a bad review or negative word of mouth can increase sales if it informs or reminds people that the product or idea exists. That's why a sixty-dollar Tuscan red wine saw sales rise by 5 percent after a prominent wine website described it as "redolent of stinky socks." It's also one reason why the Shake Weight, a vibrating dumbbell that was widely ridiculed by the media and consumers, went on to do $50 million in sales. Even negative attention can be useful if it makes products and ideas top of mind.

KIT KAT AND COFFEE: GROWING THE HABITAT

One product that used triggers brilliantly is Kit Kat.

"Give me a break, give me a break, break me off a piece of that Kit Kat bar!" Introduced in the United States in 1986, the Kit Kat tune is one of the most iconic jingles ever made. Sing the first couple of words to almost anyone over twenty-five and the person can finish the line. Researchers even deemed it one of the top ten "earworms"—a melody that gets stuck in your head—of all time. Even more memorable than "YMCA" (take that, Village People).

But in 2007, Colleen Chorak was tasked with reviving the Kit Kat brand. In the twenty-plus years since the jingle was first introduced, the brand had run out of gas. Hershey produces everything from Reese's Pieces and Hershey's Kisses to Almond

Joy, Twizzlers, and Jolly Ranchers. With this huge slate of different items, it's not surprising that a brand can get lost. And that is exactly what had happened with Kit Kat. Hershey had floundered with replacing the "give me a break" campaign. Sales were declining around 5 percent a year, and the brand had contracted considerably. People still loved the product, but consumer interest was way down.

Colleen needed a way to get consumers to start thinking about the brand again. To make Kit Kat more top of mind. And given the years of failed new directions, upper management was unwilling to spend the money to put the brand back on TV. Any financial support would be modest at best.

So she did some research. Colleen looked at when people actually consumed Kit Kats. She found two things: consumers often ate Kit Kats to take a break, and many consumed it in coordination with a hot beverage.

She had an idea.

Kit Kat and coffee.

Colleen pulled the campaign together in a matter of months. Described as "a break's best friend," the radio spots featured the candy bar sitting on a counter next to a cup of coffee, or someone grabbing coffee and asking for a Kit Kat. Kit Kat and coffee. Coffee and Kit Kat. The spots repeatedly paired the two together.

The campaign was a hit.

By the end of the year it had lifted sales by 8 percent. After twelve months, sales were up by a third. Kit Kat and coffee put Kit Kat back on the map. The then-$300 million brand has since grown to $500 million.

Many things contributed to the campaign's success. "Kit Kat and coffee" has a nice alliteration, and the idea of taking a break to have a Kit Kat fits well with the existing notion of a coffee break. But I'd like to add one more reason to the list.

Triggers. "Kit Kat and cantaloupe" is equally alliterative, and break dancing would also have fitted with the break concept. But coffee is a particularly good thing to link the brand to because it is a *frequent* stimulus in the environment. A huge number of people drink coffee. Many drink it a number of times throughout the day. And so by linking Kit Kat to coffee, Colleen created a frequent trigger to remind people of the brand.

Biologists often talk about plants and animals as having habitats, natural environments that contain all necessary elements for sustaining an organism's life. Ducks need water and grasses to eat. Deer thrive in areas that contain open spaces for grazing.

Products and ideas also have habitats, or sets of triggers that cause people to think about them.

Take hot dogs. Barbecues, summertime, baseball games, and even wiener dogs (dachshunds) are just a few of the triggers that make up the habitat for hot dogs.

Compare that with the habitat for Ethiopian food. What triggers most people to think of Ethiopian food? Ethiopian food is certainly delicious, but its habitat is not as prevalent.

Most products or ideas have a number of natural triggers. Mars bars and Mars the planet are already naturally connected. The Mars company didn't need to do anything to create that link. Likewise, French music is a natural trigger for French wine, and the last day of the workweek is a natural trigger for Rebecca Black's song "Friday."

But it's also possible to grow an idea's habitat by creating new links to stimuli in the environment. Kit Kat wouldn't normally be associated with coffee, but through repeated pairing, Colleen Chorak was able to link the two. Similarly, our trays experiment created a link between dining-room trays and a message to eat fruits and vegetables by repeatedly pairing the two ideas together. And by increasing the habitat for the message, these newly formed links helped the desired behavior catch on.

Consider an experiment we conducted with BzzAgent and Boston Market. This fast-casual restaurant is best known for home-style comfort food (rotisserie chicken and mashed potatoes) and was primarily viewed as a lunch place. Management wanted to generate more buzz. We thought we could help by growing Boston Market's habitat.

During a six-week campaign, some people were exposed to messages that repeatedly paired the restaurant with dinner. "Thinking about dinner? Think about Boston Market!". Other people received a similar advertising campaign that contained a more generic message: "Thinking about a place to eat? Think about Boston Market!" We then measured how often the respective groups talked about the restaurant.

The results were dramatic. Compared to the generic message, the message that grew the habitat (by associating Boston Market with dinner) increased word of mouth by 20 percent among people who previously had associated the brand only with lunch. Growing the habitat boosted buzz.

Competitors can even be used as a trigger.

How can public health organizations compete against the marketing strength of better-funded rivals like cigarette companies? One way to combat this inequality is to transform a weakness into a strength: by making a rival's message act as a trigger for your own.

A famous antismoking campaign, for example, spoofed Marlboro's iconic ads by captioning a picture of one Marlboro cowboy talking to another with the words: "Bob, I've got emphysema." So now whenever people see a Marlboro ad, it triggers them to think about the antismoking message.

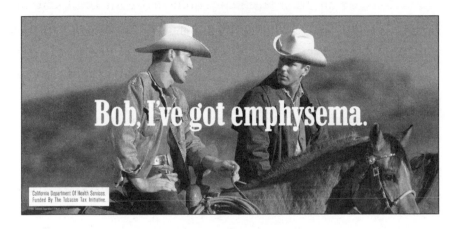

Researchers call this strategy the poison parasite because it slyly injects "poison" (your message) into a rival's message by making it a trigger for your own.

WHAT MAKES FOR AN EFFECTIVE TRIGGER?

Triggers can help products and ideas catch on, but some stimuli are better triggers than others.

As we discussed, one key factor is how *frequently* the stimulus occurs. Hot chocolate would also have fitted really well with Kit Kat, and the sweet beverage might have even complemented the chocolate bar's flavor better than coffee. But coffee is a more effective trigger because people think about and see it much more frequently. Most people drink hot chocolate only in the winter, while coffee is consumed year-round.

Similarly, Michelob ran a successful campaign in the 1970s that linked weekends with the beer brand ("Weekends are made for Michelob"). However, that wasn't the slogan when the campaign started out. Originally the slogan was "Holidays are made for Michelob." But this proved ineffective because the chosen stimuli—holidays—don't happen that often. So Anheuser-Busch revised the slogan to "Weekends are made for Michelob," which was much more successful.

Frequency, however, must also be balanced with the *strength* of the link. The more things a given cue is associated with, the weaker any given association. It's like poking a hole in the bottom of a paper cup filled with water. If you poke just one hole, a strong stream of water will gush out. But poke more holes, and the pressure of the stream from each opening lessens. Poke too many holes and you'll get barely a trickle from each.

Triggers work the same way. The color red, for example, is associated with many things: roses, love, Coca-Cola, and fast cars, to name just a few. As a result of being ubiquitous, it's not a particularly strong trigger for any of these ideas. Ask different people to say the word that first comes to their mind when they think of red and you'll see what I mean.

Compare that with how many people think "jelly" when you say "peanut butter" and it will be clear why stronger, more unusual links are better. Linking a product or idea with a stimulus that is already associated with many things isn't as effective as forging a fresher, more original link.

It is also important to pick triggers that happen near where the desired behavior is taking place. Consider a clever but ultimately ineffective public service ad from New Zealand. A handsome, muscular man is taking a shower. In the background you hear a catchy jingle about HeatFlow, a new temperature-control system that ensures you'll always have sufficient hot water for long, luxurious showers. The man turns off the water. When he opens the shower door, an attractive woman tosses him a towel. He smiles. She smiles. He begins to step out of the shower stall.

Suddenly, he slips. Falling, he cracks his head on the tile floor. As he lies there, motionless, his arm twitches slightly. A voice-over somberly intones: "Preventing slips around your home can be as easy as using a bath mat."

Wow. Definitely surprising. Extremely memorable. So memorable, I think about it every time I take a shower in a bathroom that doesn't have a mat on the floor.

But there's only one problem.

I can't buy a bath mat in a bathroom. The message is physically removed from the desired behavior. Unless I leave the bathroom, turn on my laptop, and buy a mat online, I have to remember the message until I get to a store.

Contrast that with a New York City Department of Health (DOH) antisoda campaign. While soda might seem like a relatively low-calorie item compared to all the food we eat during the course of a day, drinking sugary beverages actually has a big impact on weight gain. But the DOH didn't just want to tell people how much sugar was in soda, it wanted to make sure people would remember to change their behavior and spread the message to others.

So the DOH made a video showing someone opening what seems like a normal soda can. But when he starts to pour it into a glass, out spills fat. Blob after blob of white, chunky fat. The guy picks the glass up and knocks the fat back just as one would a regular soda—chunks and all.

The "Man Drinks Fat" clip closes with a huge congealed chunk of fat being dropped on a dinner plate. It oozes over the table as a message flashes up on the screen: "Drinking one can of soda a day can make you 10 pounds fatter a year. So don't drink yourself fat."

The video is clever. But by showing fat pouring out of a can, the DOH also nicely leveraged triggers. Unlike the bath mat ad, its video triggered the message (don't consume sugary drinks) at precisely the right time: when people are thinking of drinking a soda.

CONSIDER THE CONTEXT

These campaigns underscore how important it is to consider the context: to think about the environments of the people a message or idea is trying to trigger. Different environments contain different stimuli. Arizona is surrounded by desert. Floridians see lots of palm trees. Consequently, different triggers will be more or less effective depending on where people live.

Similarly, the effectiveness of the hundred-dollar cheesesteak that we talked about in the introduction depends on the city where it is introduced.

A hundred-dollar sandwich is pretty remarkable, wherever you are. But how frequently people will be triggered to think about it depends on geography. In places where people eat lots of cheesesteaks (Philadelphia), people would be triggered often, but in other places (such as Chicago) not so much.

Even within a given city or geographic region, people experience different triggers based on the time of day or year. One study we conducted around Halloween, for example, found that people were much more likely to think about products associated with the color orange (such as orange soda or Reese's Pieces) the day before Halloween than a week later. Before Halloween, all the orange stimuli in the environment (pumpkins and orange displays) triggered thoughts of orange products. But as soon as the holiday was over, those triggers disappeared, and so did thoughts of orange products. People moved on to thinking about Christmas or whatever holiday came next.

So when thinking about, say, how to remember to take your reusable grocery bags to the grocery store, think about what will trigger you at exactly the right time. Using reusable grocery bags is like eating more vegetables. We know we should do it. We even want to do it (most of us have bought the bags). But when it comes time to take action, we forget.

Then, right as we pull into the grocery store parking lot, we remember. Argh, I forgot the reusable grocery bags! But by then it's too late. We're at the store and the grocery bags are at home in the closet.

It's no accident that we think about reusable bags right when we get to the store. The grocery is a strong trigger for the bags. But unfortunately it is a badly timed one. Just as with the bath mat public service announcement, the idea is coming to mind, but at the wrong time. To solve this problem, we need to be reminded to bring the bags right when we are leaving the house.

What's a good trigger in this instance? Anything you have to take with you to buy groceries. Your shopping list, for example, is a great one. Imagine if every time you saw your shopping list, it made you think of your reusable bags. It would be much harder to leave the bags at home.

WHY CHEERIOS GETS MORE WORD OF MOUTH THAN DISNEY WORLD

To return to the example that started the chapter, triggers help explain why Cheerios get more word of mouth than Disney World. True, Disney World is interesting and exciting. To use the language of other chapters in the book, it has high Social Currency and evokes lots of Emotion (next chapter). But the problem is that people don't think about it very frequently. Most people don't go to Disney World unless they have kids. Even those who do go don't go that often. Once a year if that. And there are few triggers to remind them about the experience after the initial excitement evaporates.

But hundreds of thousands of people eat Cheerios for breakfast every day. Still more see the bright orange boxes every time they push their shopping carts down the supermarket cereal aisle. And these triggers make Cheerios more accessible, increasing the chance that people will talk about the product.

The number of times Cheerios and Disney are mentioned on Twitter illustrates this nicely. Cheerios are mentioned more frequently than Disney World. But examine the data closely and you'll notice a neat pattern.

Mention of Cheerios on Twitter

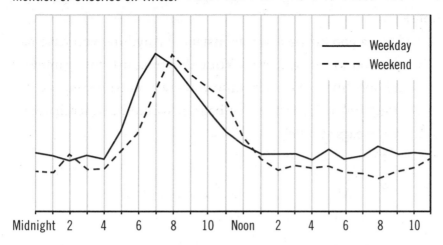

Mentions of Cheerios spike every day at approximately the same time. The first references occur at 5:00 a.m. They peak between 7:30 a.m. and 8:00 a.m. And they diminish around 11:00 a.m. This sharp increase and corresponding decline align precisely with the traditional time for breakfast. The pattern even shifts slightly on weekends when people eat breakfast later. Triggers drive talking.

Triggers are the foundation of word of mouth and contagiousness. To use an analogy, think of most rock bands. Social Currency is the front man or woman. It's exciting, fun, and gets lots of attention. Triggers could be the drummer or bassist. It's not as sexy a concept as Social Currency, but it's an important workhorse that gets the job done. People may not pay as much attention to it, but it lays the groundwork that drives success. The more something is triggered, the more it will be top of mind, and the more successful it will become.

So we need to consider the context. Like Budweiser's "was-sup" or Rebecca Black's "Friday," our products and ideas need to take advantage of existing triggers. We also need to grow the habitat. Like Colleen Chorak's Kit Kat and coffee, we need to create new links to prevalent triggers.

Triggers and cues lead people to talk, choose, and use. Social currency gets people talking, but Triggers keep them talking. Top of mind means tip of tongue.

3. Emotion

By October 27, 2008, Denise Grady had been writing about science for *The New York Times* for more than a decade. With an eye for quirky topics and a deft narrative style, Grady won numerous journalism prizes by making esoteric topics accessible to lay readers.

That day, one of Grady's articles rocketed up the newspaper's Most E-Mailed list. Within hours of its publication thousands of people had decided to pass on the article to their friends, relatives, and coworkers. Grady had scored a viral hit.

The topic? How fluid and gas dynamic theories were being used in medical research.

Grady's article detailed something called schlieren photography, in which "a small, bright light source, precisely placed lenses, a curved mirror, a razor blade that blocks part of the light beam and other tools make it possible to see and photograph disturbances in the air."

Sounds less than riveting, right? Join the club. When we asked people what they thought of this article on a number of different dimensions, the scores were pretty low. Did it have lots of

Social Currency? No, they said. Did it contain a lot of practically useful information (something we'll discuss in the Practical Value chapter)? No again.

In fact, if you'd gone down the checklist of characteristics traditionally believed to be prerequisites for viral content, Grady's article, entitled "The Mysterious Cough, Caught on Film," would have lacked most of them. Yet Grady's piece clearly had something special or so many people wouldn't have hit the e-mail button. What was it?

Grady's interest in science started in high school. She was sitting in chemistry class when she read about Robert Millikan's famous experiment to determine the charge on a single electron. It was a complicated idea and a complicated experiment. The study involved suspending tiny droplets of oil between two metal electrodes, then measuring how strong the electric field had to be in order to stop the droplets from falling.

Grady read it several times. Again and again until she finally understood. But when she did, it was like a flash going off. She got it. It was thrilling. The thinking behind the experiment was so clever, and being able to grasp it was enthralling. She was hooked.

After school Grady went to work at *Physics Today* magazine. Eventually she worked at *Discover* and *Time* magazine and finally worked her way up to health editor at *The New York Times*. The goal of her articles was always the same: to give people even just a little bit of that excitement that she had felt back in chemistry class decades before. An appreciation for the magic of scientific discovery.

In her piece that October, Grady described how an engineering professor used a photographic technique to capture a visible image of a seemingly invisible phenomenon—a human cough. The schlieren technique had been used for years by aeronautics and military specialists to study how shock waves form around high-speed aircraft. But the engineering professor had harnessed the technique in a new way: to study how airborne infections like tuberculosis, SARS, and influenza spread.

It made sense that most people thought the article wasn't particularly useful. After all, they weren't scientists studying fluid dynamics. Nor were they engineers trying to visualize complex phenomena.

And while Grady is one of the best science writers out there, it made sense that the general population would tend to be more interested in articles about sports or fashion. Finally, while coughs would certainly be a nice trigger to remind people of the article, cold and flu season tends to peak around February, four months after the article was released.

Even Grady was bemused. As a journalist, she's delighted when something she writes goes viral. And like most journalists, or even casual bloggers, she'd love to understand why some of her pieces get widely shared while others don't.

But while she could make some educated guesses, neither she nor anyone else really knew why one piece of content gets shared more than another. What made this particular article go viral?

After years of analysis, I'm happy to report that my colleagues and I have some answers. Grady's 2008 article was part of a multi-year study in which we analyzed thousands of *New York Times* articles to better understand why certain pieces of online content are widely shared.

A clue comes from the picture that accompanied Grady's

piece. Earlier that October, she had been scanning an issue of *The New England Journal of Medicine* when she came across a piece entitled "Coughing and Aerosols." As soon as she saw it she knew the research would be the perfect basis for an article in the *Times*. Some of the piece was pretty technical, with discussions of infectious aerosols and velocity maps. But above all the jargon was a simple image, an image that made Grady decide to write her article.

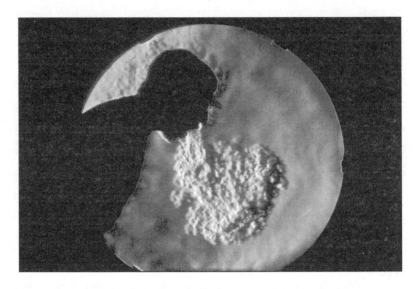

Simply put, it was amazing. The reason people shared Grady's article was *emotion*. When we care, we share.

MOST E-MAILED LISTS AND THE IMPORTANCE OF SHARING

Humans are social animals. As discussed in the chapter on Social Currency, people love to share opinions and information with others. And our tendency to gossip—for good or ill—shapes our relationships with friends and colleagues alike.

The Internet has become increasingly engineered to support these natural inclinations. If people come across a blog post about a new bike sharing program or find a video that helps kids solve tough algebra problems, they can easily hit the Share button or copy and paste the link into an e-mail.

Most major news or entertainment websites take the extra step of documenting what has been passed along most frequently. Listing which articles, videos, and other content have been most viewed or shared over the past day, week, or month.

People often use these lists as shortcuts. There is way too much content available to sift through it all—hundreds of millions of websites and blogs, billions of videos. For news alone, dozens of highly reputable outlets continuously produce new articles.

Few people have time to seek out the best content in this ocean of information. So they start by checking out what others have shared.

As a result, most-shared lists have a powerful ability to shape public discourse. If an article about financial reform happens to make the list, while one about environmental reform barely falls short, that initially small difference in interest can quickly become magnified. As more people see and share the article about financial reform, citizens may become convinced that financial reform deserves more governmental attention than environmental reform, even if the financial issue is mild and the environmental issue severe.

So why does some content make the Most E-Mailed list while other content does not?

For something to go viral, lots of people have to pass along the same piece of content at around the same time. You might have enjoyed Denise Grady's cough article, and maybe you shared it with a couple of friends. But for the piece to make the Most E-Mailed list, a large number of people had to make the same decision you did.

Is this just random? Or might there be some consistent patterns underlying viral success?

SYSTEMATICALLY ANALYZING THE MOST E-MAILED LIST

The life of a Stanford graduate student is far from grand. My office, if you could call it that, was a high-walled cubicle. It was tucked up in a windowless attic of a 1960s-era building whose architectural style has often been described as "brutalist." A short, squat structure with concrete walls so thick they could probably withstand a direct hit from a small grenade launcher. Sixty of us were clustered together in a cramped space, and my own ten-by-ten fluorescent-lit box was shared with another student.

The one upside was the elevator. Graduate students were expected to be working at all times of day and night, so the school gave us a keycard that allowed twenty-four-hour access to a special lift. Not only did it take us up to our windowless workstations, it also gave us access to the library, even after it closed. Not the most lavish perk, but a useful one.

Back then the distribution of online content was not as sophisticated as it is today. Content websites now post their most e-mailed lists online, but some newspapers published these lists in their print editions as well. Every day *The Wall Street Journal* published a list of the five most read articles and the five most e-mailed articles from the previous day's news. After scanning a couple of these lists, I was enthralled. It seemed like the perfect data source to study why some things get shared more than others.

So just as a stamp collector collects stamps, I began to collect the *Journal*'s Most Emailed list.

Once every couple of days I would use the special elevator to go hunting. I would take my trusty scissors down to the library late at night, find a stack of the most recent print editions of the *Journal,* and carefully clip out the Most Emailed lists.

After a few weeks, my collection had grown. I had a big stack of news clippings and was ready to go. I entered the lists in a spreadsheet and began looking for patterns. One day "Dealing with the Dead Zone: Spouses Too Tired to Talk" and "Disney Gowns Are for Big Girls" were two of the most e-mailed articles. A few days later "Is an Economist Qualified to Solve Puzzle of Autism?" and "Why Birdwatchers Now Carry iPods and Laser Pointers" made the list.

Hmm. On the face of it, these articles had few characteristics in common. What did tired spouses have to do with Disney gowns? And what did Disney have to do with economists studying autism? The connections were not going to be obvious.

Further, reading one or two articles at a time wasn't going to cut it. To get a handle on things I needed to work faster and more efficiently.

Luckily my colleague Katherine Milkman suggested a vastly improved method. Rather than pull this information from the print newspaper by hand, why not automate the process?

With the help of a computer programmer, we created a Web crawler. Like a never tiring reader, the program automatically scanned *The New York Times* home page every fifteen minutes, recording what it saw. Not only the text and title of each article, but also who wrote it and where it was featured (posted on the main screen or hidden in a trail of links). It also recorded in which section of the physical paper (health or business, for example) and on what page the article appeared (such as the front page or the back of the third section).

After six months we had a huge data set—every article published by *The New York Times* over that period. Almost seven thousand articles. Everything from world news and sports to health and technology, as well as which articles made the Most E-Mailed list for those same six months.

Not just what one person shared, but a measure of what all readers, regardless of their age, wealth, or other demographics, were sharing with others.

Now our analysis could begin.

First, we looked at the general topic of each article. Things like health, sports, education, or politics.

The results showed that education articles were more likely to make the Most E-Mailed list than sports articles. Health pieces were more viral than political ones.

Nice. But we were more interested in understanding what drives sharing than in simply describing the attributes of content that was shared. Okay, so sports articles are less viral than dining articles. But why? It's like saying people like to share pictures of cats or talk about paintball more than Ping-Pong. That doesn't really tell us much about why that is happening or allow us to make predictions beyond the narrow domains of cat stuff or sports that start with the letter P.

Two reasons people might share things are that they are interesting and that they are useful. As we discussed in the Social Currency chapter, interesting things are entertaining and reflect positively on the person who shares them. Similarly, as we'll discuss in the Practical Value chapter, sharing useful information helps others and makes the sharer look good in the process.

To test these theories, we hired a small army of research assistants to score *New York Times* articles on whether they contained useful information and how interesting they were. Articles about things like how Google uses search data to track the spread of the flu were scored as highly interesting, while an article about the change in the cast of a Broadway play was scored as less interesting. Articles about how to control your credit score were scored as being very useful, while the obituary of an obscure opera singer was scored as not useful. We fed these scores into a statistical analysis program that compared them with the Most E-Mailed lists.

As we expected, both characteristics influenced sharing. More interesting articles were 25 percent more likely to make the Most E-Mailed list. More useful articles were 30 percent more likely to make the list.

These results helped explain why health and education articles were highly shared. Articles about these topics are often quite useful. Advice on how to live longer and be happier. Tips for getting the best education for your kids.

But there was still one topic that stood out like a sore thumb: science articles. For the most part, these articles did not have as much Social Currency or Practical Value as articles from more mainstream sections. Yet science articles, like Denise Grady's piece about the cough, made the Most E-Mailed list more than politics, fashion, or business news. Why?

It turns out that science articles frequently chronicle innovations and discoveries that evoke a particular emotion in readers. That emotion? Awe.

THE POWER OF AWE

Imagine standing on the very edge of the Grand Canyon. The bloodred gorge stretches as far as you can see in every direction. The canyon floor drops precipitously below your feet. You feel dizzy and step back from the edge. Hawks circle through rock crevasses so barren and stripped of vegetation you could as well be on the moon. You are amazed. You are humbled. You feel elevated. This is awe.

According to psychologists Dacher Keltner and Jonathan Haidt, awe is the sense of wonder and amazement that occurs when someone is inspired by great knowledge, beauty, sublimity, or might. It's the experience of confronting something greater than yourself. Awe expands one's frame of reference and drives self-transcendence. It encompasses admiration and inspiration and can be evoked by everything from great works of art or music to religious transformations, from breathtaking natural landscapes to human feats of daring and discovery.

Awe is a complex emotion and frequently involves a sense of surprise, unexpectedness, or mystery. Indeed, as Albert Einstein himself noted, "The most beautiful emotion we can experience is the mysterious. It is the power of all true art and science. He to whom this emotion is a stranger, who can no longer pause to wonder and stand rapt in awe, is as good as dead."

More than any other emotion, awe described what many readers felt after looking at science pieces from *The New York Times*. Take "The Mysterious Cough, Caught on Film." The photo of the cough was stunning both as a visual spectacle and as an idea: that something as mundane as a cough could produce this image and yield secrets capable of solving centuries-old medical mysteries.

We decided to test whether awe drove people to share. Our research assistants went back and scored the articles based on how much awe they evoked. Articles about a new treatment for AIDS or a hockey goalie who plays even though he has brain cancer evoked lots of awe. Articles about holiday shopping bargains evoked little or no awe. We then used statistical analyses to compare these scores with whether articles were highly shared.

Our intuition was right: awe boosted sharing.

Awe-inspiring articles were 30 percent more likely to make the Most E-Mailed list. Articles previously judged to have low Social Currency and Practical Value—Grady's cough piece or an article suggesting that gorillas may, like humans, grieve when losing loved ones—nevertheless made the Most E-Mailed list because of the awe they inspired.

Some of the Web's most viral videos also evoke awe.

The snickering started as soon as the plump, matronly woman walked onto the stage. She looked more like a lunch lady than a vocalist. First, she was too old to be competing on *Britain's Got Talent.* At forty-seven, she was more than twice the age of many of the other contestants.

But, more important, she looked, well, frumpy. The other competitors were already dressed to be the next big thing. Sexy, ruggedly handsome, or hip. They wore form-fitting dresses, tailored vests, and summer scarves. But this woman looked more like an example of what not to wear. Her outfit looked like a cross between an old set of drapes and a secondhand Easter dress.

And she was nervous. When the judges started asking her questions she got stuck and stumbled on her words. "What's the dream?" they inquired. When she replied that she wanted to be a professional singer you could just see the thoughts going through their heads. That's rich! You? A professional singer? The cameras zoomed in on members of the audience laughing and rolling their eyes. Even the judges smirked. They clearly wanted her to get off the stage as soon as possible. All signs pointed to her giving a terrible performance and being booted from the show, pronto.

But just as it seemed that it couldn't get any worse, she started singing.

And time stopped.

It was breathtaking.

As the opening chords from "I Dreamed a Dream" from *Les Misérables* wafted over the speakers, Susan Boyle's exquisite voice shone through like a beacon. So powerful, so beautiful that it makes the hair on the back of your neck stand up. The judges were awed, the audience screamed, and everyone broke out into wild applause. Some started tearing up as they listened. The performance left people speechless.

Susan Boyle's first appearance on *Britain's Got Talent* is one of the most viral videos ever. In just nine short days, the clip accumulated more than 100 million views.

It's hard to watch this video and not be awed by her strength and heart. It's not only moving, it's awe-inspiring. And that emotion drove people to pass it on.

DOES ANY EMOTION BOOST SHARING?

Our initial *New York Times* findings brought up other questions. What about awe makes people share? Might other emotions have the same effect?

There are reasons to believe that experiencing any sort of emotion might encourage people to share. Talking to others often makes emotional experiences better. If we get promoted, telling others helps us celebrate. If we get fired, telling others helps us vent.

Sharing emotions also helps us connect. Say I watch a really awe-inspiring video, like Susan Boyle's performance. If I share that video with a friend, he's likely to feel similarly inspired. And the fact that we both feel the same way helps deepen our social connection. It highlights our similarities and reminds us how much we have in common. Emotion sharing is thus a bit like social glue, maintaining and strengthening relationships. Even if we're not in the same place, the fact that we both feel the same way bonds us together.

But these benefits of sharing emotion don't just arise from awe alone. They happen for all sorts of emotions.

If you send a coworker a joke that cracks both of you up, it underscores your connection. If you send your cousin an op-ed piece that makes you both angry, it strengthens the fact that you share the same views.

So would *any* type of emotional content be more likely to be shared?

To answer this, we picked another emotion, sadness, and dove back into the data. We asked our research assistants to score each article based on how much sadness it evoked. Articles about things like someone paying tribute to his deceased grandmother were scored as evoking a good deal of sadness, while articles about things like a winning golfer were scored as low sadness. If any emotion boosted sharing, then sadness—like awe—should also increase sharing.

But it didn't. In fact, sadness had the opposite effect. Sadder articles were actually 16 percent *less* likely to make the Most E-Mailed list. Something about sadness was making people less likely to share. What?

The most obvious difference between different emotions is their pleasantness or positivity. Awe is relatively pleasant, while sadness is unpleasant. Might positive emotions increase sharing, but negative emotions decrease it?

People have long speculated about how positive and negative emotions influence what people talk about and share. Conventional wisdom suggests that negative content should be more viral. Consider the old news adage "If it bleeds, it leads." This phrase is based on the notion that bad news generates more attention and interest than good news. That's why the nightly news always starts with something like: "The hidden health hazard that's lurking in your basement. Find out more, next, on the six o'clock news." Editors and producers believe that negative stories will help draw, and keep, viewers' attention.

That said, you could also make a case for the opposite: that people prefer sharing good news. After all, don't most of us want to make others feel happy or positive rather than anxious or sad? Similarly, as we discussed in the chapter on Social Currency, whether people share something often depends on how it makes them look to others. Positive things may be shared more because they reflect positively on the person doing the sharing. After all, no one wants to be Debbie Downer, always sharing things that are sad and gloomy.

So which is it? Is positive information more likely to be shared than negative, or vice versa?

We went back to our database and measured the positivity of each article. This time we used a textual analysis program developed by psychologist Jamie Pennebaker. The program quantifies the amount of positivity and negativity in a passage of text by counting the number of times hundreds of different emotional words appear. The sentence "I loved the card; that was so nice of her," for example, is relatively positive because it contains positive words like "love" and "nice." The sentence "That was so nasty of her; it really hurt my feelings," on the other hand, is relatively negative because of negative words like "hurt" and "nasty." We scored each article based on its positivity or negativity and then examined how that related to whether it made the Most E-Mailed list.

The answer was definitive: positive articles were more likely to be highly shared than negative ones. Stories about things like newcomers falling in love with New York City were, on average, 13 percent more likely to make the Most E-Mailed list than pieces that detailed things like the death of a popular zookeeper.

Finally we were feeling confident that we understood how emotion shapes transmission. It seemed like people share positive things and avoid sharing negative ones.

But just to be sure that we were correct that negative emotions decrease sharing, we gave our research assistants one final task. We asked them to score each article on two other major negative emotions: anger and anxiety.

Articles about things like Wall Street fat cats getting hefty bonuses during the economic downturn induced lots of anger, while articles about topics like summer T-shirts evoked no anger at all. Articles about things like the stock market tanking made people pretty anxious, while articles about things like Emmy Award nominees evoked no anxiety. If it were true that people share positive content and avoid sharing negative content, then anger and anxiety should, like sadness, reduce sharing.

But this wasn't the case. In fact, it was the opposite. Articles that evoked anger or anxiety were *more* likely to make the Most E-Mailed list.

Now we were really confused. Clearly, something more complicated than whether an article was positive or negative determined how widely things were shared. But what?

KINDLING THE FIRE: THE SCIENCE
OF PHYSIOLOGICAL AROUSAL

The idea that emotions can be categorized as positive or pleasant and negative or unpleasant has been around for hundreds if not thousands of years. Even a child can tell you that happiness or excitement feels good and anxiety or sadness feels bad.

More recently, however, psychologists have argued that emotions can also be classified based on a second dimension. That of activation, or physiological arousal.

What is physiological arousal? Think about the last time you gave a speech in front of a large audience. Or when your team was on the verge of winning a huge game. Your pulse raced, your palms sweated, and you could feel your heart pounding in your chest. You may have had similar feelings the last time you saw a scary movie or went camping and heard a weird noise outside your tent. Though your head kept saying you weren't really in danger, your body was convinced otherwise. Every sense was heightened. Your muscles were tensed and you were alert to every sound, smell, and movement. This is arousal.

Arousal is a state of activation and readiness for action. The heart beats faster and blood pressure rises. Evolutionarily, it comes from our ancestors' reptilian brains. Physiological arousal motivates a fight-or-flight response that helps organisms catch food or flee from predators.

We no longer have to chase our dinner or worry about being eaten, but the activation arousal provides still facilitates a host of everyday actions. When aroused we do things. We wring our hands and pace back and forth. We pump our fists in the air and run around the living room. Arousal kindles the fire.

Some emotions, like anger and anxiety, are high-arousal. When we're angry we yell at customer service representatives. When we're anxious we check and recheck things. Positive emotions also generate arousal. Take excitement. When we feel excited we want to do something rather than sit still. The same is true for awe. When inspired by awe we can't help wanting to tell people what happened.

Other emotions, however, have the opposite effect: they stifle action.

Take sadness. Whether dealing with a tough breakup or the death of a beloved pet, sad people tend to power down. They put on some cozy clothes, curl up on the couch, and eat a bowl of ice cream. Contentment also deactivates. When people are content, they relax. Their heart rates slow, and their blood pressure decreases. They're happy, but they don't particularly feel like *doing* anything. Think of how you feel after a long hot shower or a relaxing massage. You're more likely to relax and sit still than leap into another activity.

	HIGH AROUSAL	LOW AROUSAL
POSITIVE	Awe Excitement Amusement (Humor)	Contentment
NEGATIVE	Anger Anxiety	Sadness

Once we realized the important role that emotional arousal might play, we returned to our data. Just to recap, so far we had found that awe increased sharing and that sadness decreased it. But rather than finding a simple matter of positive emotions increasing sharing and negative emotions decreasing it, we found that some negative emotions, like anger or anxiety, actually increased sharing. Would physiological arousal be the key to the puzzle?

It was.

Understanding arousal helps integrate the different results we had found so far. Anger and anxiety lead people to share because, like awe, they are high-arousal emotions. They kindle the fire, activate people, and drive them to take action.

Arousal is also one reason funny things get shared. Videos about the aftereffects of a kid having anesthesia at the dentist ("David After Dentist"), a baby biting his brother's finger ("Charlie Bit My Finger—Again!"), or a unicorn going to Candy Mountain and getting his kidney stolen ("Charlie the Unicorn") are some of the most popular on YouTube. Taken together they have been viewed more than 600 million times.

But while it is tempting to say that these things went viral simply because they are funny, a more fundamental process is at work. Think about the last time you heard a really hilarious joke or were forwarded a humorous clip and felt compelled to pass it along. Just like inspiring things, or those that make us angry, funny content is shared because amusement is a high-arousal emotion.

Low-arousal emotions, however, like sadness, decrease sharing. Contentment has the same effect. Contentment isn't a bad feeling. Being content feels pretty good. But people are less likely to talk about or share things that make them content because contentment decreases arousal.

United Airlines learned the hard way that arousal can drive people to share. Dave Carroll was a pretty good musician. His group, Sons of Maxwell, wasn't a blockbuster act, but they made enough money from album sales, touring, and merchandising to pull together a decent living. People weren't tattooing Dave's name on their arms, but he was doing all right.

While traveling to a gig in Nebraska, Dave and his band had to take a connecting flight through Chicago with United Airlines. It's hard enough to find overhead space for even a small carry-on, but musicians have it even tougher. Dave's group couldn't fit their guitars in the overhead, so they had to check them with the rest of their baggage.

But as they were about to deplane at O'Hare Airport, a woman cried out, "My god, they're throwing guitars out there!" Dave looked out the window in horror just in time to see the baggage handlers roughly tossing his treasured instruments through the air.

He jumped up and pleaded with the flight attendant for help, but to no avail. One flight attendant told him to talk to the lead agent, but that agent said it wasn't her responsibility. Another employee gave him the run-around and told him to take up the matter with the gate agent when he landed in his final destination.

When Dave landed in Omaha at 12:30 a.m., he found the airport deserted. No employees in sight.

Dave made his way to baggage claim and carefully opened his guitar case. His worst fears were confirmed. His $3,500 guitar had been smashed.

But that was only the start of Dave's story. He spent the next nine months negotiating with United for some kind of compensation. He filed a claim asking United to fix the guitar, but it denied his request. Among a long list of justifications, United argued that it couldn't help him because he had missed the brief twenty-four-hour window for claiming damages described in the small print of his ticket.

Furious with the way he'd been treated, Dave channeled his emotions the way any good musician would: he wrote a song about it. He described his experience, put it to music, and posted it as a short clip on YouTube entitled "United Breaks Guitars."

Within twenty-four hours of uploading the video, he'd received almost 500 comments, most of them from other angry United customers who'd had similar experiences. In less than four days the video had more than 1.3 million views. Within ten days, more than 3 million views and 14,000 comments. In December 2009, *Time* magazine listed "United Breaks Guitars" as one of the Top 10 Viral Videos of 2009.

United appears to have felt the negative effects almost immediately. Within four days of the video being posted, its stock price fell 10 percent—the equivalent of $180 million. Although United eventually donated $3,000 to the Thelonious Monk Institute of Jazz as a "gesture of goodwill," many industry observers felt that it suffered permanent damage as a result of the incident.

FOCUS ON FEELINGS

Marketing messages tend to focus on information. Public health officials note how much healthier teens will be if they don't smoke or if they eat more vegetables. People think that if they just lay out the facts in a clear and concise way, it will tip the scales. Their audience will pay attention, weigh the information, and act accordingly.

But many times information is not enough. Most teens don't

smoke because they think it's good for them. And most people who scarf down a Big Mac and large fries and wash it down with a supersized Coke are not oblivious to the health risks. So additional information probably won't get them to change their behavior. They need something more.

And that is where emotion comes in. Rather than harping on features or facts, we need to focus on feelings; the underlying emotions that motivate people to action.

Some products or ideas may seem better suited than others for evoking emotion. It seems easier to get people excited about a new, hip lounge than logistics management. Pets and babies seem to lend themselves to emotional appeals more than banking or nonprofit financial strategy does.

But any product or service can focus on feelings, even those that don't possess any obvious emotional hook.

Take online search engines. Search engines seem like one of the least emotional products you can think of. People want the most accurate search results in the least time possible. And underneath those results is a tangle of confusing technology: link weighting, indexing, and PageRank algorithms. A difficult product to get people fired up or teary eyed about, right?

Well, Google did exactly that with its "Parisian Love" campaign.

When Anthony Cafaro graduated from New York's School of Visual Arts in 2009, he wasn't expecting to become a Googler. No one from Visual Arts had gone to work for Google before, and the company was known as a place for techies, not designers. But when Cafaro learned Google was interviewing graphic-design graduates, he thought he'd give it a shot.

The interview was a blast. By the end, the interviewers seemed less like examiners and more like old friends. Cafaro turned down a slew of offers from traditional ad agencies to join a newly formed Google design team called the Creative Lab.

After a few months, though, Anthony realized that the Creative Lab's approach wasn't exactly in line with the company's overall ethos. Great graphic design is visceral. Like art, it moves people and evokes their innermost feelings. But Google was about analytics, not emotion.

In a telling story, a designer once suggested using a certain shade of blue for the toolbar based on its visual appeal. But the product manager resisted using the color, asking the designer to justify that choice with quantitative research. At Google, colors aren't just colors, they're mathematical decisions.

The same issues came up in one of Cafaro's first projects. The Creative Lab was asked to create content to highlight the functionality of Google's new search interface. Features like finding flights, autocorrect, and language translation. One potential solution was a little tutorial on how to search better. A how-to of the different functions. Another was "A Google a Day," an online trivia game that involved using search features to solve complex puzzles.

Cafaro liked both ideas but felt something was missing. Emotion.

Google had a great interface and useful search results, but an interface doesn't make you laugh. An interface doesn't make you cry. A demo would show how the interface worked, but that would be it. Cafaro wanted to humanize the interface. He wanted not only to show features, but to move people. Build an emotional connection.

So together with the Creative Lab team, Cafaro developed a

video entitled "Parisian Love." The clip tells a budding love story, using Google searches that evolve over time. No images of people, or even voices—just the phrases entered in the search bar and the results that emerge.

It starts when a guy enters "study abroad Paris France" and clicks on one of the top search results to learn more. Later he searches for "cafés near the Louvre," and scans to find one he thinks he'll like. You hear a female laugh in the background as his next entry is "translate tu es très mignon," which he soon learns is French for "you are very cute." Quickly he then seeks advice on how to "impress a French girl," reads up on the suggestions, and searches for chocolate shops in Paris.

The music builds as the plot unfolds. We follow the searcher as he transitions from seeking long-distance relationship advice to job hunting in Paris. We see him tracking a plane's landing time and then searching for Paris churches (to the accompaniment of church bells in the background). Finally, as the music crescendos, we see him asking how to assemble a crib. The video ends with a simple message. "Search on."

You cannot watch this clip without having your heartstrings tugged. It's romantic, joyous, and inspiring all at once. I still feel tingles every time I see it, and I've watched it dozens of times.

When the Creative Lab presented the clip to the Google Search marketing team, everyone loved it. Google's CEO's wife loved it. Everyone wanted to pass it on. In fact, the clip did so well internally that Google decided to release it to the larger public. By focusing on feelings, Google turned a normal ad into a viral hit.

It doesn't require a costly ad agency or millions of dollars in focus groups to get people to feel emotion. Cafaro created the clip with four other students who had been brought in from design programs across the country. Rather than simply highlighting the latest gee-whiz feature, Cafaro's team reminded people what they love about Google Search. As one Creative Lab team member put it, "The best results don't show up in a search engine, they show up in people's lives." Well said.

In their wonderful book *Made to Stick,* Chip and Dan Heath talk about using the "Three Whys" to find the emotional core of an idea. Write down why you think people are doing something. Then ask "Why is this important?" three times. Each time you do this, note your answer, and you'll notice that you drill down further and further toward uncovering not only the core of an idea, but the emotion behind it.

Take online search. Why is search important? Because people want to find information quickly.

Why do they want to do that? So they can get answers to what they are looking for.

Why do they want those answers? So they can connect with people, achieve their goals, and fulfill their dreams. Now that's starting to get more emotional.

Want people to talk about global warming and rally to change it? Don't just point out how big the problem is or list key statistics. Figure out how to make them care. Talk about polar bears dying or how their children's health will be affected.

KINDLING THE FIRE WITH HIGH-AROUSAL EMOTIONS

When trying to use emotions to drive sharing, remember to pick ones that kindle the fire: select high-arousal emotions that drive people to action.

On the positive side, excite people or inspire them by showing them how they can make a difference. On the negative side, make people mad, not sad. Make sure the polar bear story gets them fired up.

Simply adding more arousal to a story or ad can have a big impact on people's willingness to share it. In one experiment we changed the details of a story to make it evoke more anger. In another experiment, we made an ad funnier.

In both cases, the results were the same. More anger or more humor led to more sharing. Adding these emotions boosted transmission by boosting the amount of arousal the story or ad evoked.

Negative emotions can also drive people to talk and share. Marketing messages usually try to paint products and ideas in the most positive light possible. From razors to refrigerators, ads typically show smiling customers who extol the benefits they derive from using the product. Marketers tend to avoid negative emotions out of fear they could taint the brand.

But if used correctly, negative emotions can actually boost word of mouth.

BMW kindled the fire beautifully in a 2001 campaign. The German automobile company created a series of short Internet films entitled *The Hire.* Rather than being typical feel-good commercials showing BMWs driving down various idyllic country roads, the movies were riddled with kidnappings, FBI raids, and near-death experiences. While the fear and anxiety they evoked were far from positive, the clips so highly aroused viewers that the series racked up more than 11 million views within four months. Over the same period, BMW sales increased 12 percent.

Or consider public health messages. It's often hard to put a positive spin on things when you're trying to get people to realize that smoking causes lung cancer, or that obesity reduces life expectancy by more than three years. But certain types of negative emotional appeals should be more effective in getting people to spread the word than others.

Think back to the "Man Drinks Fat" public service announcement we talked about in the Triggers chapter. A huge glob of white fat plopping down on a plate? Gross! But because disgust is a highly arousing emotion, it encouraged people to talk about and share the PSA. Designing messages that make people anxious or disgusted (high arousal) rather than sad (low arousal) will boost transmission. Negative emotions, when used correctly, can be a powerful driver of discussion.

And that brings us to babywearing.

BABYWEARING, BOYCOTTS, AND BLUNTING BAD BUZZ

The year 2008 had many firsts. The first time China hosted the Olympics, the first African American elected president of the United States, and one that you might not have been aware of. The inaugural celebration of International Babywearing Week.

The practice of carrying your baby in a sling or similar carrier has been around for thousands of years. Some experts have even argued that the practice strengthens the maternal bond, improving the health of the baby and the mother. But as strollers and other gadgets have been popularized, many parents have moved away from this practice. So in 2008, a celebration was held to raise awareness and encourage people around the world to reconsider the benefits of babywearing.

McNeil Consumer Healthcare, the maker of painkiller Motrin, saw this swell of interest as a perfect opportunity. Motrin's motto at the time was "We feel your pain." So in an attempt to show solidarity with mothers, the company created an ad centered on the aches and pains mothers can suffer from carrying their babies in slings. The ad noted that while babywearing can be great for the baby, it can put a ton of strain on the back, neck, and shoulders of the mom.

The company was trying to be supportive. It wanted to show that it understood mom's pain and Motrin was there to help. But a number of so-called mommy bloggers saw things differently. The mom's voice-over in the ad said babywearing "totally makes me look like an official mom. And so if I look tired and crazy, people will understand why."

Deeply offended on two fronts—by the implication that they wore their babies as fashion statements and that they looked crazy—mothers took to their blogs and Twitter accounts. The anger spread.

Soon thousands of people were involved. "A baby will never be a fashion statement. How outrageous is that thinking!" one cried. The posts multiplied. Many of the writers said they would boycott the company. The topic started to trend on Twitter, and the movement got picked up by *The New York Times, Ad Age,* and a host of other media outlets. Soon seven out of the top ten searches for "Motrin" and "headache" on Google referred to the marketing debacle.

Finally, after too long a delay, Motrin took the advertisement down from its website and issued a lengthy apology.

Technology has made it easier for people to organize behind a common interest or goal. By allowing people to connect quickly and easily, social media enable like-minded individuals to find one another, share information, and coordinate plans of action.

These technologies are particularly useful when people either live far apart or are dealing with an issue that has delicate political or social meaning. Many people point to social media as the catalyst behind the Arab Spring, the wave of antigovernment protests that broke out across the Arab world, eventually toppling the governments of Tunisia and Egypt, among others.

Some of these burgeoning social movements are positive. Enabling citizens to rise up against dictatorships or helping teens facing harassment to realize that life gets better.

But in other cases the comments and movements are negative in nature. False rumors may start to gain traction. Vicious gossip may circulate and build. Is it possible to predict which flare-ups will remain isolated comments and which will snowball?

Part of the answer comes back to physiological arousal. Certain types of negativity may be more likely to escalate because they evoke arousal and are thus more likely to go viral. Angry tirades about bad customer service, or anxious rumors about how a new health plan may take away benefits, should be more likely to circulate than expressions of sadness or disappointment.

So teachers and principals should be particularly wary of hurtful rumors that carry an arousing punch because they are more likely to get passed around. Similarly, Motrin's maker could have stemmed the boycott before it started by monitoring online chatter. By looking for words like "pissed off," "angry," or "mad" in people's posts, tweets, or status updates the company could have addressed unsatisfied customers before the anger built. Fixing these high-arousal emotions early can mitigate the negativity before it snowballs.

EXERCISE MAKES PEOPLE SHARE

Our emotional odyssey has one last stop.

At Wharton, we have a behavioral lab where people are paid

to do various psychology and marketing experiments. These tasks often involve clicking boxes in an online survey or circling items on a sheet of paper.

But when people came in for an experiment of mine one November a few years ago, the instructions were a bit more unusual.

Half the participants were asked to sit still in their chairs for sixty seconds and relax. Easy enough.

The other half, however, were asked to jog lightly in place for a minute. Regardless of whether they were wearing sneakers or pumps, jeans or slacks, they were asked to run in place for sixty seconds in the middle of the laboratory.

Okay. Sure. I guess. Some participants gave us a puzzled look when we made the request, but all complied.

After they were done, they participated in what seemed like a second, unrelated experiment. They were told the experimenters were interested in what people share with others and were given a recent article from the school newspaper. Then, after reading it, they were given the option of e-mailing it to anyone they liked.

In actuality, this "unrelated study" was part of my initial experiment. I wanted to test a simple but intriguing hypothesis. At this point we knew that emotionally arousing content or experiences would be more likely to be shared. But I wondered whether the effects of arousal might be even broader than that. If arousal induces sharing, then might any physiologically arousing experience drive people to share stories and information with others?

Running in place provided the perfect test. Running doesn't evoke emotion, but it is just as physiologically arousing. It gets your heart rate up, increases blood pressure, etc. So if arousal of any sort boosts sharing, then running in place should lead people to share things with others. Even if the things people are talking about or sharing have nothing to do with the reason they are experiencing arousal.

And it did. Among students who had been instructed to jog, 75 percent shared the article—more than twice as many as the students who had been in the "relaxed" group. Thus any sort of arousal, whether from emotional or physical sources, and even arousal due to the situation itself (rather than content), can boost transmission.

Understanding that arousing situations can drive people to pass things on helps shed light on so-called oversharing, when people disclose more than they should. Ever been stuck next to someone on a plane who won't stop sharing what seem like extremely personal details? Or find yourself in a conversation where later on you realize that you may have shared way more than you meant to? Why does this happen?

Sure, we may feel more comfortable with someone than we thought we would or we may have had one too many margaritas. But there is also a third reason. If situational factors end up making us physiologically aroused, we may end up sharing more than we planned.

So be careful the next time you step off the treadmill, barely avoid a car accident, or experience a turbulent plane ride. Because you've been aroused by these experiences, you may overshare information with others in the aftermath.

These ideas also suggest that one way to generate word of mouth is to find people when they are already fired up. Exciting game shows like *Deal or No Deal* or anxiety-inducing crime dramas like *CSI* are more likely to get people aroused than documentaries about historical figures. These shows should get more chatter themselves, sure, but the boosted heart rate they induce should also spill over and make people more likely to talk about the commercials that appear during the break. Ads at the gym may provoke lots of discussion simply because people are already so amped. Work groups may benefit from taking walks together because it will encourage people to share their ideas and opinions.

The same idea holds for online content. Certain websites, news articles, or YouTube videos evoke more arousal than others. Blogs about financial markets, articles about political cronyism, and hilarious videos are all likely to boost activation, which, in turn, should increase the transmission of ads or other content that appears on those pages.

Ad timing also matters. Although a show may be generally arousing, a specific scene in that show may be more activating than others. In crime shows, for example, the anxiety often peaks somewhere in the middle. When the crime is solved at the end, all tension dissipates. In game shows, excitement—and therefore arousal—is highest when contestants are about to find out how much they've won. We may end up talking more about ads that show up close to these exciting moments.

Emotions drive people to action. They make us laugh, shout, and cry, and they make us talk, share, and buy. So rather than quoting statistics or providing information, we need to focus on feelings. As Anthony Cafaro, the designer who helped develop the "Parisian Love" video at Google, noted:

> *Whether it's a digital product, like Google, or a physical product, like sneakers, you should make something that will move people. People*

don't want to feel like they're being told something—they want to be entertained, they want to be moved.

Some emotions kindle the fire more than others. As we discussed, activating emotion is the key to transmission. Physiological arousal or activation drives people to talk and share. We need to get people excited or make them laugh. We need to make them angry rather than sad. Even situations where people are active can make them more likely to pass things on to others.

Fluid dynamics and online search seem like two of the least moving topics out there. But by relating these abstract topics to people's own lives and evoking underlying emotion, Denise Grady and Anthony Cafaro got us to care, and share.

4. Public

Ken Segall was Steve Jobs's right hand man. For twelve years, Ken worked as creative director at Jobs's ad agency. He started with Apple's account in the early 1980s. When Jobs was fired and started NeXT Computer, Ken moved to be part of the project. And when Jobs returned to Apple in 1997, Ken came along as well. Ken worked on the "Think Different" campaign, was on the team that developed the "Crazy Ones" ad, and started the iCraze by naming Apple's bulbous all-in-one egg-looking desktop the iMac.

During those later years, Ken's team would sit down with Jobs every two weeks. It was a status meeting of sorts. Ken's team would share everything they were working on advertisingwise: promising ideas, new copy, and potential layouts. Jobs would do the same. He would update Ken's team on how Apple was doing, which products were selling, and whether anything new was coming down the pipeline that they might need a campaign for.

One week, Jobs approached Ken's team with a conundrum. Jobs was obsessed with the absolute best possible user experience. He always put the customer first. Customers shelled out all that money; they should be treated right. So Apple carried this mantra into all aspects of product design. From opening the box to calling for tech support. Ever notice the slow delay when you first pull the cover off the box of your new iPhone? That's because Apple has been hard at work designing that experience to provide the perfect feeling of luxury and heft.

The conundrum concerned the design of the new Power-Book G4. The laptop was going to be a marvel of technology and design. Its titanium body was revolutionary—stronger than steel yet lighter than aluminum. And, at less than one inch thick, it would be one of the thinnest laptops ever.

But Jobs wasn't concerned about the laptop's strength or weight. He was concerned about the direction of the logo.

The cover of PowerBook laptops always had a small apple with a bite taken out of the side. Consistent with their user focus, Apple wanted the logo to look right to the owner of the computer. This was particularly important given the frequency with which laptops are opened and closed. People stuff the laptops in their backpacks or bags only to pull them out later and start working. And when you pull the laptop out it's hard to know which way is up. Which side has the latch and so should face toward you when you set the laptop down on a desk or table?

Jobs wanted this experience to be as fluid as possible, so he used the logo as a compass. It faced the user when the computer was closed so that the user could easily orient the laptop when he set it down.

But the problem came when a person opened the laptop. Once the users had found a seat at the coffee shop and sat down with their macchiato, they would open their computer to start working. And once they opened the laptop the logo would flip. To everyone around them the logo would be upside down.

Jobs was a big believer in branding, and seeing all those upside-down logos wasn't a great feeling. He was even worried it might be hurting the brand.

So Jobs asked Ken's team a question. Which is more important—to have the logo look right to the customers before they opened their PowerBook, or to make it look right to the rest of the world when the laptop was in use?

As you can see the next time you glance at an Apple laptop, Ken and Jobs reversed their long-held beliefs and flipped the logo. The reason? Observability. Jobs realized that seeing others do something makes people more likely to do it themselves.

But the key word here is "seeing." If it's hard to see what others are doing, it's hard to imitate it. Making something more observable makes it easier to imitate. Thus a key factor in driving products to catch on is *public visibility*. If something is built to show, it's built to grow.

THE PSYCHOLOGY OF IMITATION

Imagine you're in an unfamiliar city. You're out of town on a business trip or vacationing with a friend and by the time you finally land, check into the hotel, and take a quick shower you're famished. It's time for dinner.

You want to go somewhere good, but you don't know the city that well. The concierge is busy and you don't want to spend a lot of time reading reviews on the Internet, so you decide to just find a place nearby.

But when you step out onto the bustling street you're struck by dozens of options. A cute Thai place with a purple awning. A hip-looking tapas bar. An Italian bistro. How do you choose?

If you're like most people you'd probably follow a time-tested rule of thumb: look for a restaurant full of people. If lots of people are eating there, it's probably good. If a place is empty, you should probably keep on walking.

This is just one example of a much broader phenomenon. People often imitate those around them. They dress in the same styles as their friends, pick entrées preferred by other diners, and reuse hotel towels more when they think others are doing the same. People are more likely to vote if their spouse votes, more likely to quit smoking if their friends quit, and more likely to get fat if their friends become obese. Whether making trivial choices like what brand of coffee to buy or important decisions like paying their taxes, people tend to conform to what others are doing. Television shows use canned laugh tracks for this reason: people are more likely to laugh when they hear others laughing.

People imitate, in part, because others' choices provide information. Many decisions we make on a daily basis are like choosing a restaurant in a foreign city, albeit with a little more information. Which one is the salad fork again? What's a good book to take on vacation? We don't know the right answer, and even if we have some sense of what to do, we're not entirely sure.

So to help resolve our uncertainty, we often look to what other people are doing and follow that. We assume that if other people are doing something, it must be a good idea. They probably know something we don't. If our tablemates seem to be using the smaller fork to pick at the arugula, we do the same. If lots of people seem to be reading that new John Grisham thriller, we buy it for our upcoming vacation.

Psychologists call this idea "social proof." This is why baristas and bartenders seed the tip jar at the beginning of their shift by dropping in a handful of ones and maybe a five. If the tip jar is empty, their customers may assume that other people aren't really tipping and decide not to tip much themselves either. But if the tip jar is already brimming with money, they assume that everyone must be tipping, and thus they should tip as well.

Social proof even plays a role in matters of life and death.

Imagine one of your kidneys fails. Your body relies on this organ to filter the toxins and waste products from your blood, but when it stops working, your whole body suffers. Sodium builds up, your bones weaken, and you're at risk of developing anemia or heart disease. If not treated quickly, you will die.

More than 40,000 people in the United States come down with end-stage renal disease every year. Their kidneys fail for one reason or another and they have two options: either go through time-consuming back-and-forth visits to a treatment center three times a week for five-hour dialysis treatments, or get a kidney transplant.

But there are not enough kidneys available for transplant. Currently more than 100,000 patients are on the wait list; more than 4,000 new patients are added each month. Not surprisingly, people on the wait list for a kidney are eager to get one.

Imagine you are on that list. It is managed on a first-come, first-served basis, and available kidneys are offered first to people at the top of the list, who usually have been waiting the longest. You yourself have been waiting for months for an available kidney. You're fairly low on the list, but finally one day you're offered a potential match. You'd take it, right?

Clearly, people who need a kidney to save their lives should take one when offered. But surprisingly, 97.1 percent of kidney offers are refused.

Now, many of those refusals are based on the kidney not being a good match. In this respect, getting an organ transplant is a bit like getting your car repaired. You can't put a Honda carburetor in a BMW. Same with a kidney. If the tissue or blood type doesn't match yours, the organ won't work.

But when she looked at hundreds of kidney donations, MIT professor Juanjuan Zhang found that social proof also leads people to turn down available kidneys. Say you are the one hundredth person on the list. A kidney would have first been offered to the first person on the list, then the second, and so on. So to finally reach you, it must have been turned down by ninety-nine other people. This is where social proof comes into play. If so many others have refused this kidney, people assume it must not be very good. They infer it is low quality and are more likely to turn it down. In fact, such inferences lead one in every ten people who refuse a kidney to do so in error. Thousands of patients turn down kidneys they should have accepted. Even though people can't communicate directly with others on the list, they make their decisions based on others' behavior.

Similar phenomena play out all the time.

In New York City, Halal Chicken and Gyro offers delicious platters of chicken and lamb, lightly seasoned rice, and pita bread. *New York* magazine ranked it as one of the top twenty food carts in the city, and people wait up to an hour to get one of Halal's tasty but inexpensive meals. Go during certain times of day and the line will stretch all the way down the block.

Now I know what you are thinking. People must wait that long because the food is really good. And you're partially right: the food is quite good.

But the same owners operate an almost identical food cart called Halal Guys right across the street. Same food, same packaging, basically an identical product. But there is no line. In fact, Halal Guys has never developed the same devout following as its sibling. Why?

Social proof. People assume that the longer the line, the better the food must be.

This herd mentality even affects the type of careers people consider. Every year I ask my second-year MBA students to do a short exercise. Half the students are asked what they thought they wanted to do with their life right when they started the MBA program. The other half are asked what they want to do *now*. Neither group gets to see the question the other was asked and responses are anonymous.

The results are striking. Before they start the MBA program, students have a broad range of ambitions. One wanted to reform the health care system, another wanted to build a new travel website, and a third wanted to get involved in the entertainment industry. Someone wanted to run for political office and another student thought about becoming an entrepreneur. A handful say they want to go into investment banking or consulting. Overall, they possess a diverse set of interests, goals, and careers paths.

The responses from students when asked what they want to do a year into the program are much more homogeneous and concentrated. More than two-thirds say they want to get into investment banking or consulting, with a small sprinkling of other careers.

The convergence is remarkable. Sure, people may learn about different opportunities during the MBA program, but part of this herding is driven by social influence. People aren't sure what career to choose, so they look to others. And it snowballs.

While less than 20 percent of people might have been interested in investment banking and consulting going into the program, that number is larger than any other career. A few people see that 20 percent and switch. A few more see those people switch, and they follow along. Soon the number is 30 percent. Which makes other people even more likely to switch. Soon that 20 percent has become much larger. So through social influence this initially small advantage gets magnified. Social interaction led students who originally preferred different paths to go in the same direction.

Social influence has a big effect on behavior, but to understand how to use it to help products and ideas catch on, we need to understand when its effects are strongest. And that brings us to Koreen Johannessen.

THE POWER OF OBSERVABILITY

Koreen Johannessen started at the University of Arizona as a clinical social worker. Originally, she was hired by the mental health group to help students deal with problems like depression and drug abuse. But after years of treating students, Johannessen realized that she was working on the wrong end of the problem. Sure, she could try to fix the ongoing issues that afflicted students, but it would be much better to prevent them before they started. So Johannessen moved over to the campus health group and took over health education, eventually becoming the director of health promotion and preventive services.

As at most universities in the United States, one of the biggest issues at Arizona was alcohol abuse. More than three-quarters of American college students under the legal drinking age report drinking alcohol. But the bigger concern was the *quantity* that students consume. Forty-four percent of students binge-drink, and more than 1,800 U.S. college students die every year from alcohol-related injuries. Another 600,000 are injured while under the influence of alcohol. It's a huge issue.

Johannessen addressed the problem head-on. She papered the campus with flyers detailing the negative consequences of bingeing. She placed ads in the school paper with information about how alcohol affects cognitive functioning and performance in school. She even set up a coffin at the student center with statistics about the number of alcohol-related deaths. But none of these initiatives seemed to put much of a dent in the problem. Simply educating students about the risks of alcohol didn't seem to be enough.

So Johannessen tried asking the students how they felt about drinking.

Surprisingly, she found that most students said they were not comfortable with the drinking habits of their peers. Sure, they might enjoy a casual drink once in a while, just like most adults. But they weren't into the heavy binge drinking they saw among other students. They spoke distastefully about the times they nursed a hungover roommate or held someone's hair while she threw up in the toilet. So while their peers seemed fine with the drinking culture, they weren't.

Johannessen was pleased. The fact that most students were against binge drinking seemed to bode well for eliminating the drinking problem—until she thought about it closely.

If most students were uncomfortable with the drinking culture, then why was it happening in the first place? Why were students drinking so much if they don't actually like it?

Because behavior is public and thoughts are private.

Put yourself in a college student's situation. When you look around, you'd *see* a lot of drinking. You'd see tailgates at the football games, keg parties at the frat house, and open bars at the sorority formal. You'd witness your peers drinking and seeming happy about it, so you'd assume that *you* are the outlier and that everyone else likes drinking more than you do. So you'd have another drink.

But what students don't realize is that *everyone* is having similar thoughts. Their peers are having the same experience. They see others drinking, so they drink, too. And the cycle continues because people can't read one another's thoughts. If they could, they'd realize that everyone felt the same way. And they wouldn't feel all this social proof compelling them to drink as much.

For a more familiar example, think about the last time you sat through a bewildering PowerPoint presentation. Something about equity diversification or supply chain reorganization. At the end of the talk, the speaker probably asked the audience if anyone had any questions.

The response?

Silence.

But not because everyone else understood the presentation. The others were probably just as bewildered as you were. But while they would have liked to raise their hands, they didn't because each one is worried that he or she is the only person who didn't understand. Why? Because no one else was asking questions. No one saw any public signal that others were confused so everyone keeps his doubts to him- or herself. Because behavior is public and thoughts are private.

The famous phrase "Monkey see, monkey do" captures more than just the human penchant for imitation. People can imitate only when they can *see* what others are doing. College students may personally be against binge drinking, but they binge because that is what they observe others doing. A restaurant might be extremely popular, but if it's hard to see inside (e.g., the front windows are frosted), there is no way passersby can use that information to inform their own choices.

Observability has a huge impact on whether products and ideas catch on. Say a clothing company introduces a new shirt style. If you see someone wearing it and decide you like it, you can go buy the same shirt, or something similar. But this is much less likely to happen with socks.

Why?

Because shirts are public and socks are private. They're harder to see.

The same goes for toothpaste versus cars. You probably don't know what kind of toothpaste your neighbors use. It's hidden inside their house, inside their bathroom, inside a cabinet. You're more likely to know what car they drive. And because car preferences are easier to observe, it's much more likely that your neighbors' purchase behavior can influence yours.

My colleagues Blake McShane, Eric Bradlow, and I tested this idea using data on 1.5 million car sales. Would a neighbor buying a new car be enough to get you to buy a new one?

Sure enough, we found a pretty impressive effect. People who lived in, say, Denver, were more likely to buy a new car if other Denverites had bought new cars recently. And the effect was pretty big. Approximately one out of every eight cars sold was because of social influence.

Even more impressive was the role of observability in these effects. Cities vary in how easy it is to see what other people are driving. People in Los Angeles tend to commute by car, so they are more likely to see what others are driving than New Yorkers, who commute by subway. In sunny places like Miami, you can more easily see what the person next to you is driving than in rainy cities like Seattle. By affecting observability, these conditions also determined the effect of social influence on auto purchases. People were more influenced by others' purchases in places like Los Angeles and Miami, where it is easier to see what others were driving. Social influence was stronger when behavior was more observable.

Observable things are also more likely to be discussed. Ever walked into someone's office or home and inquired about a weird paperweight on the desk or a colorful art print on the living room wall? Imagine if those items were locked in a safe or tucked away in the basement. Would they get talked about as much? Probably not. Public visibility boosts word of mouth. The easier something is to see, the more people talk about it.

Observability also spurs purchase and action. As we discussed in the Triggers chapter, cues in the environment not only boost word of mouth but also remind people about things they already wanted to buy or do. You may have meant to eat healthier or visit that new website your friend mentioned, but without a visible trigger to jog your memory, you're more likely to forget. The more public a product or service is, the more it triggers people to take action.

So how can products or ideas be made more publicly observable?

MAKING THE PRIVATE PUBLIC . . . WITH MOUSTACHES

Every fall I teach about sixty MBA students at the Wharton School, and by the end of October I've gotten some sense of most of the students in the class. I know who is going to be five minutes late every day, who will be the first to raise a hand, and who will be dressed like a prima donna.

So I was a bit surprised a few years ago when I walked into class in early November to see what I'd thought was a pretty buttoned-down guy sporting a big moustache. It wasn't simply that he had forgotten to shave; he had a full handlebar with ends almost ready to curl up on the sides. He looked like a cross between Rollie Fingers and a villain in an old black-and-white movie.

At first I thought he must be trying a facial hair experiment. But then when I looked around the room I noticed two other new moustache devotees. A trend seemed to be catching on. What precipitated the sudden outburst of moustaches?

Every year, cancer claims the lives of more than 4.2 million men worldwide. More than 6 million new cases are diagnosed each year. Thanks to generous donations, great headway has been made in research and treatment. But how can organizations that work to fight this disease leverage social influence to increase donations?

Unfortunately, as with many causes, whether you support a particular cancer fund is typically a private matter. If you're like most people, you probably have little idea which of your neighbors, coworkers, or even friends have donated to help fight this disease. So there is no way for their behavior to influence yours or vice versa.

And that is where the moustaches come in.

It all started one Sunday afternoon in 2003. A group of friends from Melbourne, Australia, were sitting around drinking beers.

The conversation meandered in various directions and finally ended up on 1970s and 80s fashion. "What ever happened to the moustache?" one guy asked. A few beers more and they came up with a challenge: to see who could grow the best moustache. The word spread to their other friends, and eventually they had a small group of thirty people. All grew moustaches for the thirty days of November.

Everyone had so much fun that the next November they decided to do it again. But this time they decided to put a cause behind their efforts. Inspired by the work being done with breast cancer awareness, they wanted to do something similar for men's health. So they formed the Movember Foundation and adopted the tagline "Changing the face of men's health." That year 450 guys raised $54,000 for the Prostate Cancer Foundation of Australia.

It grew from there. Next year there were more than 9,000 participants. The following year, more than 50,000. Soon the annual event started spreading around the world. In 2007, events were launched everywhere from Ireland and Denmark to South Africa and Taiwan. The organization has since raised more than $174 million worldwide. Not bad for a few tufts of facial hair.

Now, every November, men pledge to raise awareness and money by growing moustaches. The rules are simple. Start the first of the month with a clean-shaven face. For the rest of the month, grow and groom a moustache. Oh—and along the way, conduct yourself like a true country gentleman.

The Movember Foundation succeeded because they figured out how to *make the private public.* They figured out how to take support for an abstract cause—something not typically observable—and make it something that everyone can see. For the thirty days of November people who sport a moustache effectively become walking, talking billboards for the cause. As noted on Movember's website,

> *Through their actions and words they [participants] raise awareness by prompting private and public conversations around the often-ignored issue of men's health.*

And start conversation it does. Seeing someone you know suddenly sprout a moustache generates discussion. People usually gossip a bit among themselves until someone gets up the courage to ask the wearer what prompted the new facial hair. And when he explains, he shares the social currency and generates new devotees. Each year I see more and more of my students sporting moustaches come November. Making the cause public helped it catch on more quickly than it ever could have otherwise.

Most products, ideas, and behaviors are consumed privately. What websites do your coworkers like? Which ballot initiatives do your neighbors support? Unless they tell you, you may never know. And though that might not matter to you personally, it matters a lot for the success of organizations, businesses, and ideas. If people can't see what others are choosing and doing, they can't imitate them. And, like the binge-drinking college students, people might change their behavior for the worse because they feel their views aren't supported.*

---

* Making the public private is particularly important for things that people may not have originally felt comfortable talking about. Take online dating. Many people have tried it, but it is still somewhat stigmatized in the culture at large. And part of this stigma is due to the fact that people are unaware that many people they know have tried it. Online dating is relatively

Solving this problem requires making the private public. Generating public signals for private choices, actions, and opinions. Taking what was once an unobservable thought or behavior and transforming it into a more observable one.

Koreen Johannessen was able to reduce Arizona students' drinking by making the private public. She created ads in the school newspaper that merely stated the true norm. That most students had only one or two drinks, and 69 percent have four or fewer drinks, when they party. She didn't focus on the health consequences of drinking, she focused on social information. By showing students that the majority of their peers weren't bingeing, she helped them realize that others felt the same way. That most students didn't want to binge. This corrected the false inferences students had made about others' behavior and led them to reduce their own drinking as a result. By making the private public, Johannessen was able to decrease heavy drinking by almost 30 percent.

ADVERTISING ITSELF: SHARING
HOTMAIL WITH THE WORLD

One way to make things more public is to design ideas that advertise themselves.

On July 4, 1996, Sabeer Bhatia and Jack Smith introduced a new e-mail service called Hotmail. At the time, most people got their e-mail through Internet service providers like AOL. You'd

---

private behavior, so to help it catch on, online dating companies need to make people more aware how many others are doing it. Similar issues pop up in other domains. The makers of Viagra coined the term "ED" (erectile dysfunction) to get people more comfortable talking about what was once a private issue. Many colleges started a "wear jeans if you're gay" day, in part just to raise awareness and discussion for the LGBT community.

pay a monthly fee, dial up from home using a phone line, and access your messages through the AOL interface. It was restricting. You could connect only from the place where you had the service installed. You were chained to one computer.

But Hotmail was different. It was one of the first Web-based e-mail services, which allowed people to access their inbox from any computer anywhere in the world. All they needed was an Internet connection and a Web browser. Independence Day was chosen for the announcement to symbolize how the service freed people from being locked into their current provider.

Hotmail was a great product, and it also scored well on a number of the word-of-mouth drivers we've talked about so far. At the time, it was quite remarkable to be able to access e-mail from anywhere. So early adopters liked talking about it because it gave them Social Currency. The product also offered users significant benefits over other e-mail services (for starters, it was free!), so many people shared it for its Practical Value.

But the creators of Hotmail did more than just create a great product. They also cleverly leveraged observability to help their product catch on.

Every e-mail sent from a Hotmail account was like a short plug for the growing brand. At the bottom was a message and link that simply said "Get Your Private, Free E-mail from Hotmail at www.hotmail.com." Every time current Hotmail customers sent an e-mail, they also sent prospective customers a bit of social proof—an implicit endorsement for this previously unknown service.

And it worked. In a little over a year Hotmail signed up more than 8.5 million subscribers. Soon after, Microsoft bought the burgeoning service for $400 million. Since then more than 350 million users have signed up.

Apple and BlackBerry have adopted the same strategy. The signature lines at the bottom of their e-mails often say "Sent using BlackBerry" or "Sent from my iPhone." Users can easily change this default message to something else (one of my colleagues changed his signature to say "Sent by Carrier Pigeon"), but most people don't, in part because they like the Social Currency the notes provide. And by leaving these notes on their e-mail, people also help spread awareness about the brand and influence others to try it.

All these examples involve products that *advertise themselves.* Every time people use the product or service they also transmit social proof or passive approval because usage is observable.

Many companies apply this idea through prominent branding. Abercrombie & Fitch, Nike, and Burberry all garnish their products with brand names or distinctive logos and patterns. For Sale signs broadcast which Realtor the seller is working with.

Following the notion that more is better, some companies have increased the size of their logos. Ralph Lauren has always been known for its characteristic polo player, but its Big Pony shirts made this famous emblem sixteen times larger. Not to be outdone in the escalation for logo supremacy, Lacoste made a similar move. The alligator on its Oversized Croc polo shirt is so large it looks as if it will bite the arm off of any person wearing it.

But large logos aren't the only way products can advertise themselves. Take Apple's decision to make iPod headphones white. When Apple first introduced the iPod, there was lots of competition in the digital music player space. Diamond Multimedia, Creative, Compaq, and Archos all offered players, and music on one company's device couldn't easily be transferred to another. Further, it wasn't clear which, if any, of these competing standards would stick around, and whether it was worth switching from a portable CD player or Walkman to buy this new, expensive device.

But because most devices came with black headphones, Apple's white headphone cords stood out. By advertising themselves, the headphones made it easy to see how many other people were switching away from the traditional Walkman and adopting the iPod. This was visible social proof that suggested the iPod was a good product and made potential adopters feel more comfortable about purchasing it as well.

Shapes, sounds, and a host of other distinctive characteristics can also help products advertise themselves. Pringles come in a unique tube. Computers using the Microsoft operating system make a distinctive sound when they boot up. In 1992, French footwear designer Christian Louboutin felt his shoes lacked energy. Looking around, he noticed the striking red Chanel nail polish an employee was wearing. *That's it!* he thought, and applied the polish to his shoes' soles. Now Louboutin shoes always come with red-lacquered soles, making them instantly recognizable. They're distinctive and easy to see, even for people who know little about the brand.

Similar ideas can be applied to a host of products and services. Tailors give away suit bags imprinted with the tailor's name. Nightclubs use sparklers to broadcast when someone pays to get bottle service. Tickets usually sit in people's pockets, but if theater companies and minor league teams could use buttons or stickers as the "ticket" instead, "tickets" would be much more publicly observable.

Designing products that advertise themselves is a particularly powerful strategy for small companies or organizations that don't have a lot of resources. Even when there is no money to buy television ads or a spot in the local paper, existing customers can act as advertisements if the product advertises itself. It's like advertising without an advertising budget.

A product, idea, or behavior advertises itself when people consume it. When people wear certain clothes, attend a rally, or use a website, they make it more likely that their friends, coworkers, and neighbors will see what they are doing and imitate it.

If a company or organization is lucky, people consume its product or service often. But what about the rest of the time? When consumers are wearing other clothes, supporting a different cause, or doing something else entirely? Is there something that generates social proof that sticks around even when the product is not being used or the idea is not top of mind?

Yes. And it's called *behavioral residue.*

LIVESTRONG WRISTBANDS AS BEHAVIORAL RESIDUE

Scott MacEachern had a tough decision to make. In 2003, Lance Armstrong was a hot commodity. As his sponsor at Nike, MacEachern was trying to figure out the best way to harness all the attention Lance was getting.

Lance had a powerful story. Diagnosed with life-threatening testicular cancer seven years earlier, Lance had been given only a 40 percent chance of survival. But he surprised everyone not only by returning to cycling, but by coming back stronger than ever. Since his return, he had won the Tour de France an astounding five times in a row and inspired millions of people along the way. From fifteen-year-olds dealing with cancer to college students trying to stay in shape, Lance helped people to believe. If he could come back from cancer, they could overcome the challenges in their own lives. (Note that in the decade since 2003, it has become apparent that Armstrong may have achieved his success through the use of performance-enhancing drugs. But given the powerful success of Livestrong wristbands, and the Lance Armstrong Foundation more generally, it is worth considering how they became popular, outside of whether Armstrong's personal story is tainted or not.)

MacEachern wanted to capitalize on this enthusiasm. Lance had transcended sports. He had become not only a hero, but a cultural icon. MacEachern wanted to recognize Lance's achievements and celebrate his upcoming attempt at a record sixth Tour de France victory. He also wanted to use the outpouring of interest and support to raise funds and awareness for the Lance Armstrong Foundation.

MacEachern developed two potential ideas.

The first idea was a bike ride across America. People would set a mileage goal for themselves and get friends or family members to sponsor their ride. It would get more people to exercise, boost interest in cycling, and raise money for the Lance Armstrong Foundation. Lance might even do part of the trip. The event would take weeks and likely garner significant media coverage both nationally and locally in all the cities the ride covered.

The second idea was a wristband. Nike had recently begun selling Baller Bands, silicone rubber bands with inspirational messages like "TEAM" or "RESPECT" on the inside. Basketball players wore them to stay focused and increase motivation. Why not make a wristband focused on Armstrong? Nike could make 5 million of the bands, sell them for a dollar each, and give all the proceeds to the Lance Armstrong Foundation.

MacEachern liked the wristband idea, but when he pitched it to Lance's advisors they weren't convinced. The foundation thought the bands would be a dud. Bill Stapleton, Armstrong's agent, thought they had no chance of success and called them "a stupid idea." Even Armstrong was incredulous, saying, "What are we going to do with the 4.9 million that we don't sell?"

MacEachern was stuck. While he liked the wristband idea, he wasn't sure it would fly. But then he made one seemingly innocuous decision that had a big impact on the product's success. MacEachern made the wristbands yellow.

Yellow was chosen because it is the color of the race leader's jersey in the Tour de France. It's also not strongly associated with either gender, making it easy for both men and women to wear.

But it was also a smart decision from an observability perspective. Yellow is a color people almost never see.

And it is striking. Yellow stands out against almost anything people wear, making it easy to see a Livestrong wristband from far away.

This public visibility helped make the product a huge success. Not only did Nike sell the first 5 million bands, but it did so within the first six months of release. Production couldn't keep up with demand. The wristbands were such a hot item that people started bidding ten times the retail price to snag them on eBay. In the end, more than 85 million wristbands were sold. You might even know someone who wears one to this day. Not bad for a little piece of plastic.

It's hard to know how well the ride across America would have done if Nike had implemented it. And it's easy to Monday-morning-quarterback a successful strategy and say it was obviously the better choice. But regardless, one thing is clear: the wristband creates more behavioral residue than the cross-country ride ever could have. As MacEachern keenly noted:

> *The nice thing about a wristband is that it lives on. The bike ride doesn't. There'll be pictures of the bike ride and people will talk about the bike ride, but unless it goes on every year—even if it does go on every year, it doesn't live on as a reminder every day of this sort of stuff. But the wristband does.*

Behavioral residue is the physical traces or remnants that most actions or behaviors leave in their wake. Mystery lovers have shelves full of mystery novels. Politicos frame photos of themselves shaking hands with famous politicians. Runners have trophies, T-shirts, or medals from participating in 5Ks.

As discussed in the chapter on Social Currency, items like the Livestrong wristband provide insight into who people are and what they like. Even things that would otherwise be difficult to observe, like whether a person donates to a particular cause or prefers mysteries to historical fiction.

But when publicly visible, these remnants facilitate imitation and provide chances for people to talk about related products or ideas.

Take voting. It's hard to get people to turn out to vote. They have to figure out where their polling stations are located, take the morning off from work, and stand in line, sometimes for hours, until they get the chance to cast their ballots. But these hurdles are compounded by the fact that voting is a private act. Unless you actually happen to see all the people who go to the polls, you have no idea how many other people decided voting was worth the effort. So there is not much social proof.

But in the 1980s election officials came up with a nice way to make voting more observable: the "I Voted" sticker. Simple enough, but by creating behavioral residue, the sticker made the private act of voting much more public, even after people left the polling station. It provided a ready reminder that today is the day to vote, others are doing it, and you should too.

Behavioral residue exists for all types of products and ideas. Tiffany, Victoria's Secret, and a host of other retailers give customers disposable shopping bags to carry their purchases home. But because of the Social Currency associated with some of these retailers, many consumers reuse the bags rather than tossing them. They use the Victoria's Secret bags to carry their gym clothes, toss their lunch into a Tiffany bag, or use Bloomingdale's famous medium brown bag to carry papers around town. People even reuse bags from restaurants, discount stores, and other places that are not status symbols.

Clothing retailer Lululemon takes this idea one step further. Rather than make paper bags that are relatively durable, it makes shopping bags that are hard to throw away. Made of sturdy plastic like reusable grocery bags, these bags are clearly meant to be reused. So people use them to carry groceries or do other errands. But along the way this behavioral residue helps provide social proof for the brand.

Giveaways can also provide behavioral residue. Go to any conference, job fair, or large meeting where presenters have set up booths and you'll be stunned by the amount of swag they give away. Mugs, pens, and T-shirts. Beverage cozies, stress balls, and ice scrapers. A couple of years ago the Wharton School even gave me a tie.

But some of these giveaways provide better behavioral residue than others. Giving away a makeup carrying case is fine, but women usually apply makeup in the privacy of their bathrooms, so it doesn't make the brand that observable. Coffee mugs and gym bags might be used less frequently, but their use is more publicly visible.

People posting their opinions and behavior online also provide behavioral residue. Reviews, blogs, posts, or other sorts of content all leave evidence that others can find later. For this reason, many businesses and organizations encourage people to Like them—or their content—on Facebook. By simply clicking the Like button, people not only show their affinity with a product, idea, or organization, they also help spread the word that something is good or worth paying attention to. ABC News found that installing these buttons boosted its Facebook traffic by 250 percent.

Other sites push, or automatically post, what people do to their social networking pages. Music has always been a somewhat social activity, but Spotify takes this a step further. The system allows you to listen to whatever songs you like but also posts what you're listening to on your Facebook page, making it easier for your friends to see what you like (and letting them know about Spotify). Many other websites do the same.

But should we always try to make things public? Are there ever instances when making something public could be a bad idea?

ANTI-DRUG COMMERCIALS?

A sprightly, dark-haired teenager walks down the stairs of her apartment building. She's wearing a pretty silver necklace and carrying a sweater in her hand. She could be on her way to work or to meet up with a friend for coffee. Suddenly a neighbor's door opens and a voice whispers, "I got some good pot for you."

"No!" She scowls and hurries down the stairs.

A fresh-faced kid is sitting outside. He is wearing a blue sweatshirt and sports a bowl haircut that used to be popular among boys. He appears deeply engrossed in a video game when a voice interrupts him. "Cocaine?" the voice asks. "No thanks," the kid replies.

A young man is standing against a wall chewing gum. "Yo, my man, want some 'ludes?" the voice inquires. "No way!" the man exclaims, glaring back.

"Just Say No" is one of the most famous anti-drug campaigns of all time. Created by First Lady Nancy Reagan during her husband's presidency, the campaign ran public service announcements as part of a national effort to discourage teens from recreational drug use in the 1980s and 1990s.

The logic was simple. One way or another, kids are going to be asked if they want to use drugs. Whether by a friend, a stranger, or somebody else. And they needed to know how to say no. So the government spent millions of dollars on anti-drug public service announcements. It hoped that the messages would teach kids how to react in these situations and, as a result, decrease drug use.

More recent campaigns have relied on the same idea. Between 1998 and 2004, Congress appropriated almost $1 billion for the National Youth Anti-Drug Media Campaign. The goal was to educate kids ages twelve to eighteen to enable them to reject drugs.

Communications professor Bob Hornik wanted to see whether anti-drug ads were actually effective. So he collected data on the drug use of thousands of teens over the time the anti-drug ads ran. Whether teens had seen the ads and whether they had ever smoked marijuana. Then he looked at whether the public service announcements seemed to decrease marijuana use.

They didn't.

In fact, the messages actually seemed to *increase* drug use. Kids aged twelve and a half to eighteen who saw the ads were actually *more* likely to smoke marijuana. Why?

Because it made drug use more public.

Think about observability and social proof. Before seeing the message, some kids might never have thought about taking drugs. Others might have considered it but have been wary about doing the wrong thing.

But anti-drug ads often say two things simultaneously. They say that drugs are bad, but they also say that other people are doing them. And as we've discussed throughout this chapter, the more others seem to be doing something, the more likely people are to think that thing is right or normal and what they should be doing as well.

Imagine you're a fifteen-year-old who has never considered using drugs. You're sitting at home watching cartoons one afternoon when a public service announcement comes on telling you about the dangers of drug use. Someone's going to ask you if you want to try drugs and you need to be ready to say no. Or even worse, the cool kids are going to be the ones asking. But you shouldn't say yes.

You never see public service announcements for avoiding cutting off your hand with a saw or not getting hit by a bus, so if the government spent the time and money to tell you about drugs, a lot of your peers must be doing them, right? Some of them are apparently the coolest kids in school. And you had no idea!

As Hornik said,

Our basic hypothesis is that the more kids saw these ads, the more they
came to believe that lots of other kids were using marijuana. And the
more they came to believe that other kids were using marijuana, the
more they became interested in using it themselves.

As with many powerful tools, making things more public can
have unintended consequences when not applied carefully. If you
want to get people *not* to do something, don't tell them that lots of
their peers are doing it.

Take the music industry. It thought it could stop illegal
downloads by showing people how big the problem is. So the
industry association's website sternly warns people that "only 37
percent of music acquired by U.S. consumers . . . was paid for"
and that in the past few years "approximately 30 billion songs
were illegally downloaded."

But I'm not sure that message has the desired effect. If anything, it may have the opposite effect. Less than half of people are
paying for their music? Wow. Seems like you'd have to be an idiot
to pay for it then, right?

Even in cases where most people are doing the right thing,
talking about the minority who are doing the wrong thing can
encourage people to give in to temptation.

Rather than making the private public, preventing a behavior
requires the opposite: making the public private. Making others'
behavior *less* observable.

One way is to highlight what people *should* be doing instead.
Psychologist Bob Cialdini and colleagues wanted to decrease the
number of people who stole petrified wood from Arizona's Petrified Forest National Park. So they posted signs around the park
that tried different strategies. One asked people not to take the
wood because "many past visitors have removed petrified wood

from the Park, changing the natural state of the Petrified Forest."
But by providing social proof that others were stealing, the message had a perverse effect, almost doubling the number of people taking wood!

Highlighting what people should do was much more effective. Over a different set of trails they tried a different sign that stated, "Please don't remove the petrified wood from the Park, in order to preserve the natural state of the Petrified Forest." By focusing on the positive effects of *not* taking the wood, rather than on what others were doing, the park service was able to reduce theft.

It's been said that when people are free to do as they please, they usually imitate one another. We look to others for information about what is right or good to do in a given situation, and this social proof shapes everything from the products we buy to the candidates we vote for.

But as we discussed, the phrase "Monkey see, monkey do" captures more than just our tendency to follow others. If people can't see what others are doing, they can't imitate them. So to get our products and ideas to become popular we need to make them more publicly observable. For Apple this was as easy as flipping its logo. By cleverly leveraging moustaches, Movember drew huge attention and donations for men's cancer research.

So we need to be like Hotmail and Apple and design products that advertise themselves. We need to be like Lululemon and Livestrong and create behavioral residue, discernible evidence that sticks around even after people have used our product or engaged with our ideas. We need to make the private public. If something is built to show, it's built to grow.

5. Practical Value

If you had to pick someone to make a viral video, Ken Craig probably wouldn't be your first choice. Most viral videos are made by adolescents and watched by adolescents. Crazy tricks someone did on his motorcycle or cartoon characters edited to look as if they are dancing to rap songs. Things young people love.

But Ken Craig is eighty-six years old. And the video that went viral? It's about shucking corn.

Ken was born on a farm in Oklahoma, one of five brothers and sisters. His family's livelihood was built around growing cotton. They also kept a garden to grow things for the family to eat. And among those things was corn. Ken's been eating corn since the 1920s. He's eaten everything from corn casserole and corn chowder to corn fritters and corn salad. One of his favorite ways to eat corn is straight off the cob. Nice and fresh.

But if you've ever eaten corn on the cob you know that there are two problems. In addition to kernels getting stuck in your teeth, there are those pesky threadlike strands (called corn silk) that always seem stuck to the corn. A couple of strong pulls and you can easily peel the husk off, but the silk seems to cling on for dear life. You can rub the corn, carefully pick at it with tweezers, or try almost anything else you like, but whatever you do there always seem to be a couple of wayward silk strands left over.

And this is where Ken comes in.

Like most eighty-six-year-olds, Ken's not really into the Internet. He doesn't have a blog, a channel on YouTube, or any sort of online presence. In fact, to this day he has made only one YouTube video. Ever.

A couple of years ago, Ken's daughter-in-law was over at his house making dinner. She had almost finished cooking the main dish, and when it got close to time to eat, she told him that the corn was ready to be shucked. Okay, Ken said, but let me show you a little trick.

He took unshucked ears of corn and tossed them in a microwave. Four minutes an ear. Once they were done, he took a kitchen knife and cut a half inch or so off the bottom. Then he grabbed the husk at the top of the corn, gave it a quick couple of shakes, and out popped the ear of corn. Clean as a whistle. No silk.

His daughter-in-law was so impressed she said they'd have to make a video to send to her daughter who was teaching English in Korea. So the next day she shot a clip of Ken in his kitchen, talking through his trick for clean ears of corn. To make it easier for her daughter to see, she posted it on YouTube. And along the way she sent the clip to a couple of friends.

Well, those friends sent it to a couple of friends, who also sent it to a couple of friends. Soon Ken's "Clean Ears Everytime" video took off. It collected more than 5 million views.

But unlike most viral videos that skew toward young people, this one skewed in the opposite direction. Topping the charts of the videos viewed most by people above the age of fifty-five. In fact, the video might have spread even faster if more senior citizens were online.

Why did people share this video?

A couple of years ago I went hiking with my brother in the mountains of North Carolina. He was wrapping up a tough year of medical school, and I needed a break from work, so we met at Raleigh-Durham Airport and drove west. Past the Tar Heel blue of Chapel Hill, past the once tobacco-saturated city of Winston-Salem, and all the way to the Blue Ridge Mountains that hug the westernmost portion of the state. The next morning we woke up early, packed food for the day, and set out on a winding mountain ridge path that led to the top of a majestic plateau.

The main reason people go hiking is to get away from it all. To escape from the hustle and bustle of the city and to immerse themselves in nature. No billboards, no traffic, no advertising, just you and nature.

But that morning while we were hiking in the woods, we came across the most peculiar thing. As we rounded the bend on a downhill portion of the trail there was a group of hikers in front of us. We walked behind them for a couple of minutes, and being a curious guy, I happened to eavesdrop on their conversation. I thought they might be talking about the beautiful weather, or the long descent we had just covered.

But they weren't.

They were talking about vacuum cleaners.

Whether one particular model was really worth its premium price, and whether another model would do the job just as well.

Vacuum cleaners? There were thousands of other things these hikers could have talked about. Where to stop for lunch, the rushing sixty-foot falls they had just passed, even politics. But vacuum cleaners?

It's not easy to explain Ken Craig's viral corn video using the dimensions we've talked about so far in this book, but it's even harder to explain the hikers chatting about vacuum cleaners. They weren't talking about anything particularly remarkable, so Social Currency wasn't playing much of a role. While there are lots of cues for vacuums in the home, or even in a city, there aren't many Triggers for vacuum cleaners in the forest. Finally, while a clever campaign could figure out how to make vacuum cleaners more Emotional, the hikers were just having a basic conversation about features different vacuums offered. So what was driving them to talk?

The answer is simple. People like to pass along practical, useful information. News others can use.

In the context of Triggers or hidden bars like Please Don't Tell, practical value may not seem like the sexiest or most exciting concept. Some might even say it's obvious or intuitive. But that doesn't mean that it's not consequential. When writer and editor William F. Buckley Jr. was asked which single book he would take with him to a desert island, his reply was straightforward: "A book on shipbuilding."

Useful things are important.

Further, as the stories of Ken's corn and the vacuum-discussing hikers illustrate, people don't just value practical information, they share it. Offering practical value helps make things contagious.

People share practically valuable information to help others. Whether by saving a friend time or ensuring a colleague saves a couple of bucks next time he goes to the supermarket, useful information helps.

In this way, sharing practically valuable content is like a modern-day barn raising. Barns are large and costly structures that are difficult for one family to pay for or to assemble by itself. So in the eighteenth and nineteenth centuries, communities would collectively build a barn for one of their members. People would get together, volunteer their time, and help their neighbor. Next time around, the barn would be built for someone else. You can think of it as an early version of the current prosocial ideal of "pay it forward."

Today, these direct opportunities to help others are fewer and farther between. Modern suburban life has distanced us from our friends and neighbors. We live at the end of long driveways or high up in apartment buildings, often barely getting to know the person next door. Many people move away from their families for work or school, reducing face-to-face contact with our strongest social ties. Hired labor has taken the place of community barn raising.

But sharing something useful with others is a quick and easy way to help them out. Even if we're not in the same place. Parents can send their kids helpful advice even if they are hundreds of miles away. Passing along useful things also strengthens social bonds. If we know our friends are into cooking, sending them a new recipe we found brings us closer together. Our friends see we know and care about them, we feel good for being helpful, and the sharing cements our friendship.

If Social Currency is about information senders and how sharing makes them look, Practical Value is mostly about the information receiver. It's about saving people time or money, or helping them have good experiences. Sure, sharing useful things benefits the sharer as well. Helping others feels good. It even reflects positively on the sharer, providing a bit of Social Currency. But at its core, sharing practical value is about helping others. The Emotions chapter noted that when we care, we share. But the opposite is also true. Sharing is caring.

You can think about sharing practical value as akin to advice. People talk about which retirement plan is cheapest and which politician will balance the budget. Which medicine cures a cold and which vegetable has the most beta carotene. Think about the last time you made a decision that required you to gather and sift through large amounts of information. You probably asked one or more people what you should do. And they probably either shared their opinion or sent you a link to a website that helped you out.

So what makes something seem practically valuable enough to pass along?

SAVING A COUPLE OF BUCKS

When most people think about practical value, saving money is one of the first things that comes to mind—getting something for less than its original price or getting more of something than you usually would for the same price.

Websites like Groupon and LivingSocial have built business models around offering consumers discounts on everything from pedicures to pilot lessons.

One of the biggest drivers of whether people share promotional offers is whether the offer seems like a good deal. If we see an amazing deal we can't help but talk about it or pass it on to someone we think would find it useful. If the offer is just okay, though, we keep it to ourselves.

So what determines whether or not a promotional offer seems like a good deal?

Not surprisingly, the size of the discount influences how good a deal seems. Saving a hundred dollars, for example, tends to be more exciting than saving one dollar. Saving 50 percent is more exciting than saving 10 percent. You don't have to be a brain surgeon to realize that people like (and share) bigger discounts more than smaller ones.

But it's actually more complicated than that. Consider what you would do in the following example:

Scenario A: Imagine you're at a store looking to buy a new barbecue grill. You find a Weber Q 320 grill that looks pretty good, and to your delight it's also on sale. Originally priced at $350, it is now marked down to $250.

Would you buy this barbecue grill or drive to another store to look at others? Take a second to think about your answer. Got it? Okay, let's do the exercise again for a different retailer.

Scenario B: Imagine you're at a store looking to buy a new barbecue grill. You find a Weber Q 320 grill that looks pretty good and to your delight it's also on sale. Originally priced at $255, it is now marked down to $240.

What would you do in this case? Would you buy this barbecue grill or drive to another store to look at others? Wait until you have an answer and then read on.

If you're like most people, scenario A looked pretty good. One hundred dollars off a barbecue grill and it's a model you like? Seems like a good deal. You probably said you'd buy it rather than keep looking.

Scenario B, however, probably didn't look so good. After all, it's only fifteen dollars off, nowhere near as good as the first deal. You probably said you'd keep looking rather than buy that one.

I found similar results when I gave each scenario to one hundred different people. While 75 percent of the people who received scenario A said they'd buy the grill rather than keep looking, only 22 percent of people who received scenario B said they'd buy the grill.

This all makes perfect sense—until you think about the final price at each store. Both stores were selling the same grill. So if anything, people should have been more likely to say they would buy it at the store where the price was lower (scenario B). But they weren't. In fact, the opposite happened. More people said they would purchase the grill in scenario A, even though they would have had to pay a higher price ($250 rather than $240) to get it. What gives?

THE PSYCHOLOGY OF DEALS

On a cold, wintry day in December 2002, Daniel Kahneman walked onstage to address a packed lecture hall at Sweden's Stockholm University. The audience was filled with Swedish diplomats, dignitaries, and some of the world's most prominent academics. Kahneman was there to give a talk on bounded rationality, a new perspective on intuitive judgment and choice. He had given related talks over the years, but this one was slightly different. Kahneman was in Stockholm to accept the Nobel Prize in Economics.

The Nobel Prize is one of the world's most prestigious awards and is given to researchers who have contributed great insight to their disciplines. Albert Einstein received a Nobel Prize for his work on theoretical physics. Watson and Crick received a Nobel in medicine for their work on the structure of DNA. In economics, the Nobel Prize is awarded to a person whose research has had a large impact on advancing economic thinking.

But Kahneman isn't an economist. He is a psychologist.

Kahneman received the Nobel for his work with Amos Tversky on what they called "prospect theory." The theory is amazingly rich, but at its core, it's based on a very basic idea. The way people actually make decisions often violates standard economic assumptions about how they *should* make decisions. Judgments and decisions are not always rational or optimal. Instead, they are based on psychological principles of how people perceive and process information. Just as perceptual processes influence whether we see a particular sweater as red or view an object on the horizon as far away, they also influence whether a price seems high or a deal seems good. Along with Richard Thaler's work, Kahneman and Tversky's research is some of the earliest studying what we now think of as "behavioral economics."

One of the main tenets of prospect theory is that people don't evaluate things in absolute terms. They evaluate them relative to a comparison standard, or "reference point." Fifty cents for coffee isn't just fifty cents for coffee. Whether that seems like a fair price or not depends on your expectations. If you live in New York City, paying fifty cents for a cup of coffee seems pretty cheap. You'd chuckle at your good luck and buy coffee from that place every day. You might even tell your friends.

If you live in rural India, though, fifty cents might seem hugely expensive. It would be way more than you would dream of paying for coffee and you'd never buy it. If you told your friends anything it would be your outrage at the price gouging.

You see the same phenomenon at work if you go to the movies or the store with people in their seventies or eighties. They often complain about the prices. "What?" they exclaim. "No way am I paying eleven dollars for a movie ticket. That's such a rip-off!"

It might seem that old people are stingier than the rest of us. But there is a more fundamental reason that they think the prices are unfair. They have different reference points. They remember the days when a movie ticket was forty cents and steak was ninety-five cents a pound, when toothpaste was twenty-nine cents and paper towels cost a dime. Because of that, it's hard for them to see today's prices as fair. The prices seem so much higher than what they remember, so they balk at paying them.

Reference points help explain the barbecue grill scenarios we discussed a few pages ago. People use the price they expect to pay for something as their reference point. So the grill seemed like a better deal when it was marked down from $350 to $250 rather than when it was discounted from $255 to $240, even though it was the same grill. Setting a higher reference point made the first deal seem better even though the price was higher overall.

Infomercials often use the same approach.

The amazing Miracle Blade knives last forever! Watch them slice through a pineapple, soda can, or even a penny! You might expect to pay $100 or even $200 for a set of knives like these, but right now you can get this incredible knife set for only $39.99!

Sound familiar? It should. Most infomercials use this technique to make whatever they are offering seem like a great deal. By mentioning $100 or $200 as the price you might expect to pay, the infomercial sets a high reference point, making the final price of $39.99 seem like a steal.

This is also why retailers often list a "regular" or manufacturer's standard retail price even when something is on sale. They want consumers to use those prices as the reference price, making the sale price look even better. Consumers are so focused on getting a good deal that, as the barbecue grill example showed, they sometimes even end up paying more to get it.

Reference points also work with quantities.

But wait, there's more! If you call now, we'll throw in a second set of these knives absolutely free! That's right, an extra set for the same price. And we'll even throw in this handy knife sharpener. No extra charge!

Here the infomercial is taking the reference quantity and augmenting it. You expected to pay $39.99 for one set of Miracle Blade knives, but now you are getting an extra set, and a knife sharpener, for the same price. In addition to the price being lower than your expectations (which was set by them in the first place), the additional goods makes the offer seem like an even better deal.

How far will the effect of putting something on sale go? Marketing scientists Eric Anderson and Duncan Simester wanted to find out. So a few years ago they paired up with a company that sends clothing catalogs to homes across the United States. Think L.L. Bean, Spiegel, or Lands' End. Most of the clothes in these catalogs are full price, but sometimes the catalog features certain sale items and drops its prices. Not surprisingly, this increases sales. People like to pay less, so dropping the price makes things more desirable.

But Anderson and Simester had a different question in mind.

They wondered whether consumers find the idea of a discount so powerful that merely labeling something as "on sale" would increase purchase.

To test this possibility, Anderson and Simester created two different versions of the catalog and mailed each to more than fifty thousand people. In one version some of the products (let's call them dresses) were marked with signs that said "Pre-Season SALE." In the other version the dresses were not marked as on sale.

Sure enough, marking those items as on sale increased demand. By more than 50 percent.

The kicker?

The prices of the dresses were the same in both versions of the catalog. So using the word "sale" beside a price increased sales *even though the price itself stayed the same.*

Another tenet of prospect theory is something called "diminishing sensitivity." Imagine you are looking to buy a new clock radio. At the store where you expect to buy it, you find that the price is $35. A clerk informs you that the same item is available at another branch of the same store for only $25. The store is a twenty-minute drive away and the clerk assures you that they have what you want there.

What would you do? Would you buy the clock radio at the first store or drive to the second store?

If you're like most people, you're probably willing to go to the other store. After all, it's only a short drive away and you save almost 30 percent on the radio. It seems like a no-brainer.

But consider a similar example. Imagine you are buying a new television. At the store where you expect to buy it, you find that the price is $650. A clerk informs you that the same item is available at another branch of the same store for only $640. The store is a twenty-minute drive away and the clerk assures you that they have what you want there.

What would you do in *this* situation? Would you be willing to drive twenty minutes to save $10 on the television?

If you're like most people, this time around you probably said no. Why drive twenty minutes to save a few bucks on a TV? You'd probably spend more on gas than what you'd save on the product. In fact, when I gave each scenario to one hundred different people, 87 percent said they'd buy the television at the first store while only 17 percent said the same for the clock radio.

But if you think about it, these two scenarios are essentially the same. They're both about driving twenty minutes to save $10. So people should have been equally willing to take the drive in each scenario.

Except they weren't. While almost everyone is willing to endure the drive for the cheaper clock radio, almost no one is willing to do it when buying a TV. Why?

Diminishing sensitivity reflects the idea that the same change has a smaller impact the farther it is from the reference point. Imagine that you enter a lottery at your office or your child's school. You're not expecting to get much out of it, but to your surprise you win $10. Lucky you! Winning anything is great, so you'd probably be pretty happy about it.

Now imagine you won $20 instead. You'd probably feel even happier. Maybe you wouldn't be doing backflips in either case, but winning $20 would feel significantly better than winning only $10.

Okay, now let's take that same lottery and that same $10 increase in winnings and let's raise the stakes a little. Imagine you won $120 rather than $110. Or even better, $1,020 rather than $1,010. Suddenly that extra $10 wouldn't matter as much. You'd probably feel essentially the same if you won $120 rather than $110. If you won $1,020 rather than $1,010 you probably wouldn't even notice. The same change—gaining ten more dollars—has a smaller and smaller impact the farther you move from your reference point of zero dollars or not winning anything.

Diminishing sensitivity helps explain why people are more willing to drive to save the money on the clock radio. The clock radio was much cheaper, so a discount from $35 to $25 seems like a pretty good deal. But even though the television is also $10 off, it doesn't seem like a bargain given how much more expensive the television was in the first place.

HIGHLIGHTING INCREDIBLE VALUE

Deals seem more appealing when they highlight incredible value. As discussed in the Social Currency chapter, the more remarkable something is, the more likely it will be discussed. We're bombarded with deals all the time. If we shared every time the grocery store knocked ten cents off a can of soup no one would be friends with us anymore. A deal needs to cut through the clutter to get shared.

As prospect theory illustrates, one key factor in highlighting incredible value is what people expect. Promotional offers that seem surprising or surpass expectations are more likely to be shared. This can be because the actual deal itself exceeds expectations (for example, the percentage off is so unbelievable) or because the way the deal is framed makes it seem that way.

Another factor that affects whether deals seem valuable is their availability. Somewhat counterintuitively, making promotions more restrictive can actually make them more effective. Just as in the examples of Please Don't Tell and Rue La La that we discussed in the Social Currency chapter, restricting availability through scarcity and exclusivity makes things seem more valuable.

Take timing or frequency. Putting something on sale can make it seem like a good deal. But if a product is always on sale people start to adjust their expectations. Rather than the full, "regular" price being their reference point, the sale price becomes the expected price. This happens with rug stores that always offer 70 percent off. People come to realize that "sales" are the norm and no longer see them as deals. The same is true even with the word "sale." While noting something is on sale can increase demand, if too many items in a store are listed as being on sale, it can actually reduce purchase.

But offers that are available for only a limited time seem more appealing because of the restriction. Just like making a product scarce, the fact that a deal won't be around forever makes people feel that it must be a really good one.

Quantity limits work the same way. Retailers sometimes create limits around the number of a given discounted item a given customer can buy. "One per household" or "Limit three per customer." You might think that by making it harder for people to get as many as they want these restrictions would hurt demand. But they actually have the opposite effect by making the promotion seem like an even better deal. "Wow, if I can only get one of these, it must mean that the deal is so good that the store is worried about running out of them. Better get one fast!" Indeed, research finds that quantity purchase limits increase sales by more than 50 percent.

Even restricting who has access can make a promotional offer seem better. Some deals are available to everyone. Anyone can walk up to the discount rack at the Gap and get money off chinos, just as any patron can take advantage of happy hour at his or her local pub. But other deals are customized, or restricted to a certain set of customers. Hotels reward loyal members with "exclusive" hotel rates and restaurants have "soft openings" for a certain clientele.

These offers seem special. This boosts sharing not only by increasing Social Currency, but also by making the deal itself seem better. Like restrictions on quantity or timing, the mere fact that not everyone can get access to this promotion makes it seem more valuable. This increases Practical Value, which in turn, boosts sharing.

The Rule of 100

Another framing factor that impacts practical value is how promotional offers are expressed. Some offers are expressed in dollars off, or absolute discounts ($5 or $50 off). Other offers are expressed in percentage off, or relative discounts (5 percent or 50 percent off). Could whether a promotion is framed as money or as a percentage off affect how big the discount seems?

Take twenty percent off a $25 shirt. The same reduction can be represented as 20 percent off or $5 off. Which seems like a better deal?

Or think about a $2,000 laptop. The same reduction on a $2,000 laptop can be represented as 10 percent off or $200 off. Does one method of framing the discount make the deal seem better than the other?

Researchers find that whether a discount seems larger as money or percentage off depends on the original price. For low-priced products, like books or groceries, price reductions seem more significant when they are framed in percentage terms.

Twenty percent off that $25 shirt seems like a better deal than $5 off. For high-priced products, however, the opposite is true. For things like laptops or other big-ticket items, framing price reductions in dollar terms (rather than percentage terms) makes them seem like a better offer. The laptop seems like a better deal when it is $200 off rather than 10 percent off.

A simple way to figure out which discount frame seems larger is by using something called the Rule of 100.

If the product's price is less than $100, the Rule of 100 says that percentage discounts will seem larger. For a $30 T-shirt or a $15 entrée, even a $3 discount is still a relatively small number. But percentagewise (10 percent or 20 percent), that same discount looks much bigger.

If the product's price is more than $100, the opposite is true. Numerical discounts will seem larger. Take a $750 vacation package or the $2,000 laptop. While a 10 percent discount may seem like a relatively small number, it immediately seems much bigger when translated into dollars ($75 or $200).

So when deciding how good a promotional offer really is, or how to frame a promotional offer to make it better, use the Rule of 100. Think about where the price falls relative to $100 and how that shifts whether absolute or relative discounts seem more attractive.

One last point about promotional offers is that the practical value is more effective the easier it is for people to see. Take the shopper discount cards that you get at your local grocery store or pharmacy. These cards are certainly useful. They save consumers money and sometimes even give them free gifts if they have accumulated enough purchases. But one problem is that the practical value is not very visible. The only information people get about how much they saved is hidden among a half dozen other pieces of information on a lengthy receipt. And given that most people don't show their receipts to others, it's unlikely that anyone but the person who used the card will see how much they saved. That makes it less likely that the information will be contagious.

But what if stores made the practical value easier to see? They could put up a sign at checkout that shows other people in line how much the person checking out saved. Or the store might ring a bell every time someone saved more than twenty-five dollars. This would make two things happen. First, people would get a better sense of how much they could save by getting the card, encouraging anyone who doesn't have one yet to get one. Second, it would allow people to see the impressive amounts that some other shoppers were able to save, encouraging them to transmit these remarkable stories of practical value. As discussed in the Public chapter, it's hard to talk about something you can't see.

MORE THAN MONEY

I am terrible at investing. Too many options, too much daily volatility, and too much risk. I'd rather keep my money in a cardboard box under my bed than put it in some mutual fund that could lose money. The first time I bought stocks I barely dipped my toe in. I picked two or three that seemed like good long-term investments based on being strong brands and tried to leave it at that.

But my curiosity got the best of me. I frantically checked every day how each stock was doing. A dollar up today? Huge success! Thirty-five cents down the next day? Hopelessly despondent and considering giving up investing ever again.

Needless to say I needed help. So when it came time to put

money in my 401(k) for work, I picked some safe index funds that track the stock market.

Soon after, Vanguard, the firm that manages my retirement plan, sent me a short e-mail asking if I'd like to receive its monthly newsletter, *MoneyWhys*. Like most people, I try to avoid signing up for new mailing lists, but this one actually seemed useful. Last-minute tax tips, responses to common questions about investing, and an answer (or at least an opinion) on that age-old question of whether money can really buy happiness. I signed up.

Now, once a month, Vanguard sends me a short e-mail with useful information about financial management. One month it was tips on what homeowner's insurance actually covers. Another month it provided tips on using your PC to track personal finances.

To be honest, I don't read every e-mail Vanguard sends (sorry, Vanguard), but I end up forwarding many of the ones I do read to people I know who I think will find them useful. I sent the piece about homeowner's insurance to a colleague who just bought a home. I forwarded the piece about tracking personal finances to a friend who is trying to become more fiscally responsible. Vanguard nicely packages its expertise into a short, tight bundle of useful information, and the practical value made me pass it along. And along the way I'm spreading the word about Vanguard and its investment expertise.

Useful information, then, is another form of practical value. Helping people do things they want to do, or encouraging them to do things they should do. Faster, better, and easier.

As we discussed in the Emotions chapter, our analysis of *The New York Times* Most E-Mailed list found that articles about health and education were some of the most frequently shared.

Recipes and reviews of up-and-coming restaurants were also highly shared. One reason is that these types of articles all provide useful information. The health section suggests solutions for people with hearing loss and techniques for boosting mental fitness in middle age. The education section covers useful programs for teens and provides insight into the college admissions process. Sharing this type of content with others enables them to eat, live, and learn better.

Look at the content you've been e-mailed over the past few months and you'll see similar patterns. Articles about sunscreen brands that *Consumer Reports* rated the best, tips to recover quickly from exercise, or hints for great pumpkin carving design around Halloween. All these things are *useful*. Practical advice is shareable advice.

In thinking about why some useful content gets shared more, a couple of points are worth noting. The first is how the information is packaged. Vanguard doesn't send out a rambling four-page e-mail with twenty-five advice links about fifteen different topics. It sends out a short, one-page note, with a key header article and three or four main links below it. It's easy to see what the main points are, and if you want to find out more, you can simply click on the links. Many of the most viral articles on *The New York Times* and other websites have a similar structure. Five ways to lose weight. Ten dating tips for the New Year. The next time you're waiting in the checkout line at the grocery store, take a look at the magazines and you'll see the same idea being applied. Short lists focused around a key topic.

A cosmetic manufacturer makes a helpful iPhone application for business travelers. In addition to providing local weather information, it also provides expert skin care advice that is tailored to those local conditions. Humidity, rain, and air quality affect your hair and skin, so the application tells you the right way to respond. This practically valuable information not only is useful, but also demonstrates the company's knowledge and expertise in this domain.

The second key is the audience. Some stories or information have a broader audience than others. In the United States, at least, more people follow professional football than follow water polo. Similarly, you probably have more friends that like American restaurants than like Ethiopian restaurants.

You might think that content that has a broader audience is more likely to be shared. A piece about football should be shared more than one about water polo; a review about a new American restaurant should be passed on more than a review of a new Ethiopian place. After all, people have way more friends with whom they could share the article, so shouldn't it end up reaching more people overall?

The problem with this assumption, though, is that just because people *can* share with more people doesn't mean they will. In fact, narrower content may actually be more likely to be shared because it reminds people of a specific friend or family member and makes them feel compelled to pass it along. You might have a lot of friends who like American food or football. But because so many people are interested in that type of thing, no one person strongly comes to mind when you come across related content. In contrast, you may have only one friend who cares about Ethiopian restaurants or water polo, but if you read an article about those topics you think about your friend right away. And because it seems so uniquely perfect for her, you feel you *have* to share it.

So while broadly relevant content could be shared more, content that is obviously relevant to a narrow audience may actually be more viral.

A NOTE ON TRUTH

You may have heard that vaccines cause autism. If so, you're not alone. In 1998, a paper was published in a medical journal suggesting that an immunization against measles, mumps, and rubella could cause autism in children. Health-related news spreads fast, particularly when it relates to kids, and soon lots of people were talking about the potential downsides to vaccines. As a result, childhood vaccination rates decreased.

All this would be good if the link between vaccines and autism were true. But it's not. There is no scientific evidence that vaccines cause autism. The original paper turned out to be a fraud. The doctor who authored it had manipulated evidence, apparently owing to conflict of interest, and after being found guilty of serious professional misconduct, lost his medical license. But even though the information was false, lots of people shared it.

The reason is practical value. People weren't trying to share false things, they just heard something they thought was useful and they wanted others' kids to be safe. But many people didn't hear the news that the original report had been discredited, and so they continued to share an incorrect narrative. Our desire to share helpful things is so powerful that it can make even false ideas succeed. Sometimes the drive to help takes a wrong turn.

So the next time someone tells you about a miracle cure, or warns about the health risks of a particular food or behavior, try to verify that information independently before you pass it on. False information can spread just as quickly as the truth.

Practical value is about helping. This chapter discussed the mechanics of value and the psychology of deals, but it's important to remember why people share that type of information in the first place. People like to help one another. We go out of our way to give advice or send others information that will make them better off. Sure, some of this may be selfish. We think we're right and we can't help but toss our two cents into other people's lives. But not all of it is about us. It's also about altruism, the inherent goodness of people. We care about others and we want to make their lives better.

Of the six principles of contagiousness that we discuss in the book, Practical Value may be the easiest to apply.

Some products and ideas already have lots of Social Currency, but to build it into a video for a blender takes some energy and creativity. Figuring out how to create Triggers also requires some effort, as does evoking emotion. But finding Practical Value isn't hard. Almost every product or idea imaginable has something useful about it. Whether it saves people money, makes them happier, improves health, or saves them time, all of these things are news you can use. So thinking about why people gravitate to our product or idea in the first place will give us a good sense of the underlying practical value.

The harder part is cutting through the clutter. There are lots of good restaurants and helpful websites, so we need to make our product or idea stand out. We need to highlight incredible value and use the Rule of 100. Like Vanguard, we need to package our knowledge and expertise so that people learn about us while they pass it along. We need to make it clear why our product or idea is so useful that people just have to spread the word. News you can use.

6. Stories

The war had raged for ten long years, with no finish in sight. According to legend, Odysseus devised a cunning plan to end the fruitless siege. The Greeks built a giant wooden horse and hid their best warriors inside. The rest of their army then sailed away, pretending to return to their homeland and leaving the monumental horse behind on the beach.

The Trojans found the horse and dragged it into Troy as a symbol of their victory. They tied ropes around the beast's neck and dozens of men set huge log rollers underneath the wooden body to pull it slowly up from the beach. Others worked to take down the gate so that the monstrous sculpture could be dragged inside the city walls.

Once the statue was inside, the Trojans celebrated the end of the decade-long conflict. They decorated the temples with greenery, unearthed the jugs of sacrificial wine, and danced to rejoice at the conclusion of their ordeal.

But that night, while the city lay unconscious in drunken slumber, the Greeks sprang from their hiding place. They slid to the ground, silenced the sentries, and opened the huge gates to the city. The rest of the Greek army sailed back under the cover of darkness and soon joined them, easily walking through the very gates they had fruitlessly assaulted for so many years.

The city was able to stand a decade of battle, but it could not withstand an attack from within. Once inside, the Greeks destroyed the town, decisively ending the Trojan War.

The story of the Trojan Horse has been passed on for thousands of years. Scientists and historians estimate that the battle took place around 1170 BC, but the story was not written down until many years later. For centuries the tale was transmitted orally as an epic poem, spoken or sung to music.

The story reads like a modern-day reality show. It's full of twists and turns that include personal vendettas, adultery, and double crosses. Through a potent mixture of drama, romance, and action, it holds listeners' interest.

But the story of the Trojan Horse also carries an underlying message: "Beware of Greeks bearing gifts." A more general interpretation would be "never trust your enemies, even when they seem friendly." In fact it is exactly *when* they are making such overtures that you should be especially suspicious. So the tale of the Trojan Horse is more than just an entertaining story. It also teaches an important lesson.

Still, if Homer and Virgil had simply wanted to teach people a lesson, couldn't they have done it more efficiently? Couldn't they have gotten right to the point rather than writing an epic poem with hundreds of lines of poetry?

Of course. But would the lesson have had the same impact? Probably not.

By encasing the lesson in a story, these early writers ensured that it would be passed along—and perhaps even be believed more wholeheartedly than if the lesson's words were spoken simply and plainly. That's because people don't think in terms of information. They think in terms of *narratives*. But while people focus on the story itself, information comes along for the ride.

STORIES AS VESSELS

Stories are the original form of entertainment. Imagine you were a Greek citizen in 1000 BC. There was no Internet. No *SportsCenter* or six o'clock news. No radio or newspapers. So if you wanted entertainment, stories were the way to get it. The Trojan Horse, *The Odyssey,* and other famous tales were the entertainment of the day. People would gather round a fire, or sit in an amphitheater, to hear these epic narratives told again and again.

Narratives are inherently more engrossing than basic facts. They have a beginning, middle, and end. If people get sucked in early, they'll stay for the conclusion. When you hear people tell a good story you hang on every word. You want to find out whether they missed the plane or what they did with a house full of screaming nine year olds. You started down a path and you want to know how it ends. Until it does, they've captured your attention.

Today there are thousands of entertainment options, but our tendency to tell stories remains. We get together around our proverbial campfires—now water coolers or girls'/guys' night out—and tell stories. About ourselves and the things that have happened to us lately. About our friends and other people we know.

People tell stories for the same reasons they share word of mouth. Some narratives are about Social Currency. People tell the story of going through the phone booth to get into Please Don't Tell because it makes them look cool and in the know. Other stories are driven by (high arousal) Emotion. People tell the story of *Will It Blend?* because they are amazed that a blender could shred marbles or an iPhone. Practical Value also plays a role. People share the story of how their neighbor's dogs got sick after eating a certain type of chew toy because they want your dog to avoid the same fate.

People are so used to telling stories that they create narratives even when they don't actually need to. Take online reviews. They're supposed to be about product features. How well a new digital camera worked and whether the zoom is as good as the company suggests. But this mostly informational content often ends up being embedded in a background narrative.

> *My son just turned eight so we were planning our first trip to Disney World last July. We needed a digital camera to capture the experience so bought this one because my friend recommended it. The zoom was great. We could easily get sharp pictures of Cinderella's Castle even from far away.*

We're so used to telling stories that we do it even when a simple rating or opinion would have sufficed.

Just like the Trojan Horse itself, stories are more than they seem. Sure, the outward shell of a story—we could call this the surface plot—grabs your attention and engages your interest. But peel back that exterior, and you'll usually find something hidden inside. Underneath the star-crossed lovers and thundering heroes there is usually something else being conveyed.

Stories carry things. A lesson or moral. Information or a take-home message. Take the famous story "The Three Little Pigs." Three brothers leave home to head into the world to seek their fortune. The first little pig quickly builds his house out of straw. The second pig uses sticks. Both throw their houses together as quickly as possible so they can hang out and play the rest of the day. The third pig, however, is more disciplined. He takes the time and effort to carefully build his house out of bricks, even while his brothers have fun around him.

One night, a big bad wolf comes along looking for something to eat. He goes to the first pig's house and says those words so beloved by small children: "Little pig, little pig, let me in." But when the pig says no, the wolf blows the pig's house down. He does the same to the house of sticks. But when the wolf tries the same thing at the third pig's house, it doesn't work. He huffs and he puffs but the wolf can't destroy the third pig's house because it's made of bricks.

And that's the moral of the story. Effort pays off. Take the time to do something right. You might not have as much fun right away, but you'll find that it's worth it in the end.

Lessons or morals are also embedded in thousands of other fairy tales, fables, and urban legends. "The Boy Who Cried Wolf" warns about the dangers of lying. "Cinderella" shows that being good to others pays off. Shakespeare's plays carry valuable lessons about character and relationships, power and madness, love and war. These are complex lessons, but they are instructive nevertheless.

The ordinary stories we tell one another every day also carry information.

Take the story of the coat my cousin bought from Lands' End. He'd moved from California to the East Coast a couple of years ago, and in preparation for his first real winter he went to a fancy department store and bought a nice topcoat. The coat was one of those three-quarter-length wool varieties that men often wear over suits. It fitted well, the color was perfect, and my cousin felt like a dapper English gentleman.

There was only one problem. It wasn't warm enough. It was great when the temperature outside was in the fifties and even the forties, but once the temperature got down to the thirties the cold seeped right through the coat into my cousin's bones.

After one winter of looking great but freezing every day on his way to work, he decided it was time to get a real winter coat. He even decided to go whole hog and get one of those goose-down numbers that make you look as if you're wearing a sleeping bag—the kind of coat that is ubiquitous in the East and Midwest but never seen in California. So he went online, found a great deal at Lands' End, and bought a down commuter coat rated to minus thirty degrees Fahrenheit. Warm enough to withstand even the coldest East Coast winter.

My cousin really liked the coat, and indeed it was super warm. But halfway through the season he broke the zipper. Ripped it right off the lining. He was devastated. He had just bought the coat a few months before and it was broken already. How much would it cost to have it fixed? And how long would he have to wait to get it back from being repaired?

It was mid-January, not a very ideal time to be walking around without a winter coat.

So he called Lands' End. How much will it cost to repair, he asked, and how long will it take to be fixed?

My cousin braced for the icy reply he was used to getting from customer service people. It always seems to be the customer's problem. So sorry to hear the product broke or the service isn't working, customer service people usually say, but unfortunately it's not our fault. It's outside the warranty or you tried to do something beyond the normal use. But we'd be happy to repair it for twice the cost of the product or send someone out to check on it. Just as long as you can stay home from work for the three-hour window during which we may or may not show up. Oh, and by the way, the script the brand consultants wrote reminds us to tell you that we *really* appreciate your business.

But to his surprise, the Lands' End customer service person said something entirely different. "Repair?" she asked. "We'll just send you a new one in the mail." "How much will that cost?" my cousin asked nervously. "It's free," she replied, "and we'll send it out two-day mail so you don't have to wait. It's too cold this winter to go out with a broken coat."

A free replacement sent right away if a product breaks? Wow! That's almost unheard of in this day and age of "the customer is always wrong." Remarkable customer service. Customer service the way it is supposed to be. My cousin was so impressed he just had to tell me what happened.

My cousin's experience makes for a nice story, but when you look closer there is also a huge amount of useful information hidden in the narrative: (1) Topcoats look great but aren't really warm enough for a bitter East Coast winter. (2) Down coats make you look like a mummy, but they're worth getting if you want to stay warm. (3) Lands' End makes a really warm winter coat. (4) It also has outstanding customer service. (5) If something goes wrong, Lands' End will fix it. These are just a handful of the nuggets of knowledge woven into a deceptively simple story.

The same is true for most stories people tell us. How we

avoided the traffic jam or how the dry cleaner was able to take our oil-splattered white shirt and make it look like new. These stories contain helpful information: a good route to take if the highway is blocked; a great dry cleaner if you need to get out tough stains.

Stories, then, can act as vessels, carriers that help transmit information to others.

LEARNING THROUGH STORIES

Stories are an important source of cultural learning that help us make sense of the world. At a high level, this learning can be about the rules and standards of a group or society. How should a good employee behave? What does it mean to be a moral person? Or on a more basic level: who's a good mechanic who won't overcharge?

Beyond stories, think about other ways that people could acquire this information. Trial and error might work, but it would be extremely costly and time-consuming. Imagine if finding an honest mechanic required taking your car to two dozen different places around town and getting work done at each one. It would be exhausting (and expensive).

Alternatively, people could try direct observation, but that's also tough. You'd have to cozy up to the mechanics in all the different shops and convince them to let you watch what they did and tell you how much they charged. Guess how well that would work.

Finally, people could get their information from advertisements. But ads aren't always trustworthy, and people are generally skeptical of persuasion attempts. Most ads for mechanics will say they have great prices and do good work, but without really checking, it's hard to know for sure.

Stories solve this problem. They provide a quick and easy way for people to acquire lots of knowledge in a vivid and engaging fashion. One good story about a mechanic who fixed the problem without charging is worth dozens of observations and years of trial and error. Stories save time and hassle and give people the information they need in a way that's easy to remember.

You can think of stories as providing proof by analogy. There is no way to be sure that if I buy something from Lands' End, I'll get the same wonderful customer service my cousin received. But the mere fact that it happened to someone who is like me makes me feel that there is a pretty good chance it will happen to me too.

People are also less likely to argue against stories than against advertising claims. Lands' End representatives could tell us that they have great customer service, but as we discussed earlier, the fact that they are trying to sell something makes it difficult to believe them. It's harder to argue with personal stories.

First, it's hard to disagree with a specific thing that happened to a specific person. What is someone going to tell my cousin, "No, I think you're lying, there's no way Lands' End would be that nice"? Hardly.

Second, we're so caught up in the drama of what happened to so-and-so that we don't have the cognitive resources to disagree. We're so engaged in following the narrative that we don't have the energy to question what is being said. So in the end, we're much more likely to be persuaded.

People don't like to seem like walking advertisements. The Subway sandwich chain offers seven subs with less than six grams of fat. But no one is going to walk up to a friend and just spit out that information. Not only would it be weird, it would be out of context. Sure, this information is practically valuable if someone is trying to lose weight, but unless weight loss is the topic of conversation, or the situation triggers people to think about ways to lose weight, they're not going to bring it up. So the fact that Subway has a bunch of low-fat options may not be brought up that often.

Contrast that with the Jared story. Jared Fogle lost 245 pounds eating Subway sandwiches. Bad eating habits and lack of exercise led Jared to balloon to 425 pounds in college. He was so heavy that he picked his courses based on whether the classroom had large-enough seats for him to be comfortable rather than whether he liked the material.

But after his roommate pointed out that his health was getting worse, Jared decided to take action. So he started a "Subway diet": almost every day he ate a foot-long veggie sub for lunch and a six-inch turkey sub for dinner. After three months of this self-imposed regimen he had lost almost 100 pounds.

But he didn't stop there. Jared kept up his diet. Soon his pants size had dropped from an enormous sixty inches to a normal thirty-four-inch waist. He lost all that weight and had Subway to thank.

The Jared story is so entertaining that people bring it up even when they're not talking about weight loss. The amount of weight he lost is impressive, but even more astonishing is the fact that he lost it eating Subway sandwiches. A guy loses 245 pounds eating fast food? The summary alone is enough to draw people in.

The story gets shared for many of the reasons we talked about in prior chapters. It's remarkable (Social Currency), evokes surprise and amazement (Emotion), and provides useful information about healthy fast food (Practical Value).

People don't talk about Jared because they want to help Subway, but Subway still benefits because it is part of the narrative. Listeners learn about Jared, but they also learn about Subway along the way. They learn that (1) while Subway might seem like fast food, it actually offers a number of healthy options. (2) So healthy that someone could lose weight by eating them. (3) A lot of weight. Further, (4) someone could eat mostly Subway sandwiches for three months and still come back for more. So the food must be pretty tasty. Listeners learn all this about Subway, even though people tell the story because of Jared.

And that is the magic of stories. *Information travels under the guise of what seems like idle chatter.*

BUILD A TROJAN HORSE

Stories thus give people an easy way to talk about products and ideas. Subway might have low-fat subs, and Lands' End might have great customer service, but outside of triggers in a conversation, people need a reason to bring that information up. And good stories provide that reason. They provide a sort of psychological cover that allows people to talk about a product or idea without seeming like an advertisement.

So how can we use stories to get people talking?

We need to build our own Trojan Horse—a carrier narrative that people will share, while talking about our product or idea along the way.

Tim Piper never had a sister. And he grew up going to an all-boys school. So he had always thought it was a little ridiculous

that so many of his girlfriends had beauty issues. They were always worried that their hair was too straight, their eyes were too
light, or their complexion wasn't clear enough. Piper didn't get it.
They seemed pretty enough to him.

But after interviewing dozens of girls, Piper started to realize
that the media were to blame. Advertising, and the media in general, taught young women that something was wrong with them.
That they needed fixing. And after years of being bombarded
with those messages, women started to believe them.

What would help women realize that these ads were fake?
That the images being shown didn't reflect reality?

One night his girlfriend at the time was putting on makeup to
go out when it hit him. He realized that girls needed to be exposed
to the before *before* the after. What models look like before the
makeup and hair styling and retouching and Photoshop swoop in
to make them "perfect."

So he created a short film.

Stephanie stares into the camera and nods her head to the
crew that she is ready to begin. She is pretty, but not in a way that
would make her stand out in a crowd. Her hair is dark blond,
feathered, and relatively straight. Her skin is nice but a few blem-
ishes mar it here and there. She looks as though she could be
anyone—your neighbor, your friend, your daughter.

A bright light turns on, and the process begins. As we watch,
makeup artists darken Stephanie's eyes and highlight her lips with
gloss. They apply foundation to her skin and blush to color her
cheeks. They groom her eyebrows and lengthen her lashes. They
curl and tease and style her hair.

Then the photographer appears with his camera. He takes
dozens of photos. Fans are turned on so her hair appears naturally

tousled. Stephanie alternately smiles and stares provocatively at the camera. Finally, the photographer gets a shot he likes.

But getting the perfect snapshot is only the beginning. Next comes the Photoshopping. Stephanie's image is fed into a computer, and begins to morph before our eyes. Her lips are inflated. Her neck is thinned and lengthened. Her eyes are enlarged. These are only a handful of the dozens of changes that are made.

You are now gazing at a snapshot of a supermodel. As the camera pans backward, you can see that the image has been placed on a billboard for a makeup campaign. The screen fades to black, and small words appear in white writing. "No wonder our perception of beauty is distorted."

Wow. This is a powerful clip. A great reminder of all that really goes on behind the scenes in the beauty industry.

But in addition to being a great conversation piece, it's also a clever Trojan Horse for Dove products.

The media in general, and the beauty industry in particular, tend to paint a skewed picture of women. Models are usually tall and skinny. Magazines show women with flawless complexions and perfect teeth. Ads scream that their products can transform you into a better you. Younger face, fuller lips, softer skin.

Not surprisingly, these messages have a hugely negative impact on how women see themselves. Only 2 percent of women describe themselves as beautiful. More than two-thirds believe that the media has set an unrealistic standard of beauty that they'll never be able to achieve. No matter how hard they try. This feeling of not living up to expectations even affects young girls. Dark-haired girls wish they were blond. Redheads hate their freckles.

Piper's video, entitled "Evolution," gives a behind-the-scenes look at what goes into making the images we are bombarded with every day. It reminds people that these stunning-looking women are not real. They are fantasies, fictions only loosely based on actual people. Concocted using all the magic that digital editing can provide. The clip is as raw and shocking as it is thought provoking.

But the film wasn't sponsored by concerned citizens or an industry watchdog group. Piper made the film in coordination with Dove, maker of health and beauty products, as part of its "Campaign for Real Beauty." This was Dove's effort to celebrate the natural physical variations we all have and then to inspire women to be confident and comfortable with themselves. Another ad for soap featured real women of all shapes and sizes, rather than the rail-thin models people are used to seeing.

Not surprisingly, the campaign sparked a great deal of discussion. What does it mean to be beautiful? How are the media shaping these perceptions? What can we do to make it better?

The campaign created more than just controversy. In addition to making the issue more Public, and giving people an excuse to talk about a topic that would have otherwise been private, the campaign also got them thinking, and talking, about Dove.

The company was commended for using real people in its campaigns and for getting people to talk about this complicated but important issue. And "Evolution," which cost only a little over one hundred thousand dollars to make, got more than 16 million views. It netted the company hundreds of millions of dollars in exposure. The clip won numerous industry awards and more than tripled the website traffic the company received from Dove's 2006 Super Bowl ad. Dove experienced double-digit sales growth.

"Evolution" was widely shared because Dove latched onto something people already wanted to talk about: unrealistic beauty norms. It's a highly emotional issue, but something so controversial that people might have been afraid to bring up otherwise. "Evolution" brought it out in the open. It let people air their grievances and think about solutions. And along the way the brand benefited. Dove got people talking by starting a conversation about beauty norms—but the brand was smuggled in as part of the discussion. By creating an emotional story, Dove created a vessel that carried its brand along for the ride.

And that brings us to the story of Ron Bensimhon.

MAKING VIRALITY VALUABLE

On August 16, 2004, Canadian Ron Bensimhon carefully shed his warm-up pants and stepped to the edge of the three-meter springboard. He had attempted dives from this height many times before, but never during an event of this magnitude. It was the Athens Olympics. The world's biggest stage for sport and the pinnacle of athletic competition. But Ron did not seem fazed. He shook off the jitters and raised his hands high above his head. As the crowd roared, he leapt off the end of the board and completed a full belly flop.

A belly flop? In the Olympics? Surely Ron must have been devastated. But as he emerged from the water he seemed calm, happy even. He swam around for a few moments, hamming it up for the audience and then slowly swam to the side of the pool, where he was met by a platoon of Olympic officials and security guards.

Ron had broken into the Olympics. He wasn't actually on the Canadian swim team. In fact, he wasn't an Olympic athlete at all. He was the self-proclaimed most famous streaker in the world, and he had crashed the Olympics as part of a publicity stunt.

When Ron jumped off the springboard, he wasn't naked, but he wasn't wearing swim trunks either. He wore a blue tutu and white polka dot tights. And emblazoned across his chest was the name of an Internet casino, GoldenPalace.com.

This wasn't the first Golden Palace publicity stunt (though the company did say that Ron's stunt was done without its knowledge). In 2004 it bid $28,000 on eBay for a grilled cheese sandwich that some people believed displayed an image of the Virgin Mary. In 2005 it gave a woman $15,000 to change her name to GoldenPalace.com. But the stunt with the "fool in the pool," as Bensimhon has been called, was one of the biggest. Millions of people were watching, and the story got picked up by news outlets around the world. It also got a huge amount of word-of-mouth chatter. Someone crashing the Olympics and diving into a pool in a tutu? What a story. Pretty remarkable.

But as the days ticked by, people didn't talk about the casino. Sure, some people who saw Bensimhon's jump went to the website to try to figure out what was going on. But most people who shared the story talked about the stunt, not the website. They talked about whether the interruption threw off the Chinese divers, who flubbed their final dive right after the trick and lost the gold medal. They talked about security at the Olympics and how someone could slip through so easily at such a major event. And they talked about Bensimhon's trial and whether he would serve jail time.

What they didn't talk about was GoldenPalace.com. Why?

Marketing experts talk about "the fool in the pool" as one of the worst guerrilla marketing failures of all time. Usually they deride it for having disrupted the competition and ruining the moment for athletes who had trained all their lives. They also point out that it led to Bensimhon being arrested and fined. These are all good reasons to consider Bensimhon's belly flop, well, a flop.

But I'd like to add another one to the list. The stunt had nothing to do with the product it was trying to promote.

Yes, people talked about the stunt, but they didn't talk about the casino. Polka dot tights, tutus, and breaking into the Olympics to dive into a pool are all great story material. That's why people talked about them. So if the goal was to get people to think more about security at the Olympics or get attention for a new style of tights, the stunt succeeded.

But it had nothing to do with casinos. Not even in the slightest.

So people talked about the remarkable story but left the casino out because it was irrelevant. They might have mentioned that Bensimhon was sponsored by someone but didn't mention the casino either because it was so irrelevant that they forgot, or because it didn't make the story any better. It's like building a magnificent Trojan Horse but forgetting to put anything inside.

When trying to generate word of mouth, many people forget one important detail. They focus so much on getting people to talk that they ignore the part that really matters: *what people are talking about.*

That's the problem with creating content that is unrelated to the product or idea it is meant to promote. There's a big difference between people talking about content and people talking about the company, organization, or person that created that content.

Evian's famous "Roller Babies" video had the same problem. The clip shows what appear to be diaper-wearing babies doing tricks on roller skates. They jump over one another, hop over fences, and do synchronized moves, all to the beat of the song "Rapper's Delight." The babies' bodies are clearly animated, but their faces look real, making the video remarkable to watch. The video got more than 50 million views, and *Guinness World Records* declared it the most viewed online advertisement in history.

But while you might think that all this attention would benefit the brand, it didn't. That same year Evian lost market share and sales dropped almost 25 percent.

The problem? Roller-skating babies are cute, but they have nothing to do with Evian. So people shared the clip, but that didn't benefit the brand.

The key, then, is to not only make something viral, but also make it valuable to the sponsoring company or organization. Not just virality but *valuable virality.*

Take Barclay Prime's hundred-dollar cheesesteak that we talked about at the beginning of the book. Compared with dancing babies and bottled water, an expensive, high-end cheesesteak and an expensive, high-end steak restaurant are clearly more related. And the item wasn't just a stunt, it was an actual option on Barclay's menu. Further, it directly spoke to the inferences the restaurant wanted consumers to make about its food: high quality but not stuffy, lavish but creative.

Virality is most valuable when the brand or product benefit is *integral* to the story. When it's woven so deeply into the narrative that people can't tell the story without mentioning it.

One of my favorite examples of valuable virality comes from the Egyptian dairy company Panda, which makes a variety of different cheese products.

The commercials always start innocuously: workers talking about what to have for lunch, or a hospital nurse checking in on a patient. In one spot a father is grocery shopping with his son. "Dad, why don't we get some Panda cheese?" the son asks as they walk by the dairy aisle. "Enough!" the father replies. "We have enough stuff in the cart already."

Then the panda appears. Or rather, a man in a panda suit. There's simply no way to describe adequately the ludicrousness of this moment. Yes, a giant panda is suddenly standing in the middle of a grocery store. Or in a different commercial, an office. Or in another, a medical clinic.

In the grocery-store video, the father and son stare at the panda, obviously dumbfounded. As a Buddy Holly tune plays, the boy and his father look at the Panda cheese on the shelf, then back to the panda. And back and forth again. The father gulps.

Then, pandemonium ensues (excuse the pun).

The panda slowly walks toward the shopping cart, calmly places both hands on its sides, and flips it over.

Food flies all over the aisle—pasta, canned goods, and liquids everywhere. The stare-down continues as the father and the panda stand on opposite ends of the cart. A long pause ensues. Then the panda kicks the overturned food for good measure. "Never say no to Panda," a voice intones as a panda hand flashes the product on the screen.

The commercial and others like it are impeccably timed and utterly hilarious. I've shown them to everyone from college kids to financial service executives and everyone laughs until their sides hurt.

But note that what makes these videos so great is not just that they're funny. The commercial would have been just as funny if the guy was dressed in a chicken suit or if the tagline was, "Never say no to Jim's used cars." Someone dressed in an animal suit kicking groceries is funny regardless of which animal it is or what product it's for.

They're successful—and great examples of valuable virality—because the brand is an integral part of the stories. Mentioning the panda is a natural part of the conversation. In fact, you'd have to try pretty hard not to mention the panda and still have the story make sense (much less get people to understand why it's funny). So the best part of the story and the brand name are perfectly intertwined. That increases the chance not only that people telling the story will talk about Panda the brand, but also that they will remember what product the commercial is for, days or even weeks later. Panda is part and parcel of the story. It's an essential part of the narrative.

The same can be said for Blendtec's *Will It Blend?* campaign. It's impossible to tell the story of the clips where the blender tears through an iPhone without talking about a blender. And without recognizing that the Blendtec blender in the videos must be extremely tough—so strong that it can blend almost anything. Which is exactly what Blendtec wants to communicate.

In trying to craft contagious content, valuable virality is critical. That means making the idea or desired benefit a key part of the narrative. It's like the plot of a good detective story. Some details are critical to the narrative and some are extraneous. Where were the different suspects at the time of the murder? Critical. What was the detective eating for dinner while he mulled over the details of the case? Not so important.

The same distinction can be applied to the content we've been discussing. Take Ron Bensimhon's Olympic stunt. Jumping into a pool? Critical. GoldenPalace.com? Pretty much irrelevant.

The importance of these different types of details becomes even clearer when people retell the story. Think about the story of the Trojan Horse. It has survived for thousands of years. There is a written account of the story, but most of the details people know come from hearing someone else talk about it. But which details people remember and retell? It isn't random. Critical details stick around, while irrelevant ones drop out.

Psychologists Gordon Allport and Joseph Postman examined a similar issue more than fifty years ago. They were keenly interested in what happened to rumors as they spread from person to person. Did the stories stay the same as they were transmitted or did they change? And if they changed, were there predictable patterns in how rumors evolved?

To address this question, they had people play what most of us would describe as a game of Telephone.

First, someone was shown a picture of a detailed situation—in one case, a group of people on a subway car. The car appears to be an Eighth Avenue Express and it is going past Dyckman Street. There are various advertisements posted on the car, and five people are seated, including a rabbi and a mother carrying her baby. But the focus of the picture is two men having an argument. They are standing up, and one is pointing at the other and holding a knife.

Then the game of Telephone starts. The first person (transmitter) is asked to describe the picture to someone else (receiver), who cannot see it. The transmitter conveys the various details as he sees fit. The transmitter then leaves the room and a new person enters. That new person becomes the receiver, and the original receiver becomes the transmitter, sharing what happened in the image with the new receiver, who also hasn't seen the image. Then the original receiver leaves the room, a new person enters, and the game is repeated to a fourth, fifth, and eventually sixth person. Allport and Postman then looked at which story details persisted along the transmission chain.

They found that the amount of information shared dropped dramatically each time the rumor was shared. Around 70 percent of the story details were lost in the first five to six transmissions.

But the stories didn't just become shorter: they were also sharpened around the main point or key details. Across dozens of transmission chains there were common patterns. Certain details were consistently left out and certain details were consistently retained. In the story about the subway car the first person telling the story mentioned all the details. They talked about how the subway car seemed to be an Eighth Avenue Express, how it was going past Dyckman Street, and how there were a number of people on it, two of them arguing.

But as the story was passed on down the telephone line, many of the unimportant details got stripped out. People stopped talking about what type of subway it was or where it was traveling and instead focused on the argument. The fact that one person was pointing at the other and brandishing a knife. Just as in the detective story, people mentioned the critical details and left out the extraneous ones.

If you want to craft contagious content, try to build your own Trojan Horse. But make sure you think about valuable virality.

Make sure the information you want people to remember and transmit is critical to the narrative. Sure, you can make your narrative funny, surprising, or entertaining. But if people don't connect the content back to you, it's not going to help you very much. Even if it goes viral.

So build a Social Currency–laden, Triggered, Emotional, Public, Practically Valuable Trojan Horse, but don't forget to hide your message inside. Make sure your desired information is so embedded into the plot that people can't tell the story without it.

Epilogue

Ask three people where they got their last manicure, and chances are good that at least one of them had a Vietnamese nail technician. But the story of how it got that way might surprise you. It started with twenty women and a set of long coral nails.

She'd been a high school teacher in her home country, but when Thuan Le arrived at Hope Village in 1975, she had nothing but the clothes on her back. The tent city outside Sacramento was a holding ground for Vietnamese refugees who escaped to America after the fall of Saigon. Teeming with new immigrants, the camp simultaneously brimmed with hope and despair. People had come to America with dreams of a better life for themselves and their families, but with little English knowledge, so the possibilities were limited.

Actress Tippi Hedren, who had starred in Alfred Hitchcock's *The Birds,* was drawn to the refugees' plight and would visit Hope Village every few days. Hedren wanted to help, so she became a mentor to some of the women. Former business owners, teachers, and government officials in Vietnam, these industrious women were eager to get to work. Hedren was enchanted by their stories of Vietnam. They, in turn, noticed something about her: her beautiful nails.

The women admired Hedren's glossy light pink fingernails, so she brought her manicurist in once a week to give them lessons. How to trim cuticles, wrap nails, and remove calluses. The women were quick studies and practiced on Hedren, themselves, and anyone they could get their hands on.

Soon a plan was hatched. Hedren got the women free classes at a nearby beauty school. They learned how to file, paint, and trim. Then Hedren asked around and helped Le and the other women find jobs in Santa Monica and surrounding cities.

It was tough at first. Manicures were not yet the rage and there was lots of competition. But Le and the other women passed their licensing exams and started doing business. They worked hard, labored long hours, and took the jobs no one else wanted. The women were diligent and kept at it. They made money and worked their way up.

Seeing Le's success, a few of her friends decided to get into the business. They opened one of the first beauty salons owned by Vietnamese Americans and encouraged others to do the same.

The success stories soon spread. The thousands of Vietnamese who came to the United States looking for new possibilities heard what others were doing, and they listened. Vietnamese nail salons started opening up all around Sacramento. Then through the rest of California. Then the entire country. These twenty women started the trend, but soon it had a life of its own.

Today, 80 percent of manicurists in California are Vietnamese Americans. Nationwide the number is greater than 40 percent.

Vietnamese nail salons became contagious.

———

The story of Thuan, Tippi, and the spread of Vietnamese nail salons is pretty amazing. But even more surprising is the fact that it's not unique.

Other immigrant groups have cornered similar niches. Estimates suggest that Cambodian Americans own approximately 80 percent of the doughnut shops in Los Angeles, and that Koreans own 65 percent of the dry cleaners in New York City. In the 1850s, 60 percent of the liquor stores in Boston were run by Irishmen. In the early 1900s, Jews produced 85 percent of men's clothes. The list goes on.

When you think about it, these stories make a lot of sense. People move to a new country and start looking for work. But while the immigrants may have had various skilled jobs previously, their options in the new country are often limited. There is a language barrier, it's tough to transfer previous certifications or qualifications, and they don't have as many contacts as they had back home. So immigrants look to their friends and acquaintances for help.

And as with the rest of the products and ideas we've talked about throughout the book, social influence and word of mouth kick in. The topic of employment is frequent among new immigrants looking for work (Triggers). So they look to see what jobs other recent immigrants have taken (Public) and talk to them about the best opportunities. These more established immigrants want to look good (Social Currency) and help others (Practical Value) so they tell exciting (Emotion) narratives (Stories) about others they know who have been successful.

Soon these new immigrants follow their peers and pursue the same line of work.

———

The story of Vietnamese manicurists, and immigrants' choice of occupations more generally, highlights a number of points we've discussed throughout the book.

First, any product, idea, or behavior can be contagious. We've talked about blenders (*Will It Blend?*), bars (Please Don't Tell), and breakfast cereals (Cheerios). "Naturally" exciting products, like discount shopping (Rue La La) and high-end restaurants (Barclay Prime's hundred-dollar cheesesteak) and less traditionally buzz-worthy goods like corn (Ken Craig's "Clean Ears Everytime") and online search (Google's "Parisian Love"). Products (iPod's white headphones) and services (Hotmail) but also nonprofits (Movember and Livestrong bands), health behaviors ("Man Drinks Fat"), and whole industries (Vietnamese nail salons). Even soap (Dove's "Evolution"). Social influence helps all sorts of products and ideas catch on.

Second, we saw that rather than being caused by a handful of special "influential" people, social epidemics are driven by the products and ideas themselves.

Sure, every great story has a hero. Tippi Hedren helped Vietnamese women learn about manicures, and George Wright had the creative idea that started *Will It Blend?* But while these individuals provided the initial spark, they're only one small part of the story. Describing why a small handful of cool or connected people (so-called influentials) are not as important to social epidemics as we might think, sociologist Duncan Watts makes a nice comparison to forest fires. Some forest fires are bigger than others, but no one would claim that the size of the fire depends on the exceptional nature of the initial spark. Big forest fires aren't caused by big sparks. Lots of individual trees have to catch fire and carry the flames.

Contagious products and ideas are like forest fires. They can't happen without hundreds, if not thousands, of regular Joes and Janes passing the product or message along.

So why *did* thousands of people transmit these products and ideas?

And that's where we get to the third point: certain characteristics make products and ideas more likely to be talked about and shared. You might have thought it was just random why some things catch on, that certain products and ideas just got lucky. But it's not just luck. And it's not a mystery. The same key principles drive all sorts of social epidemics. Whether it's about getting people to save paper, see a documentary, try a service, or vote for a candidate, there is a recipe for success. The same six principles, or STEPPS, drive things to catch on.

Social Currency	We share things that make us look good
Triggers	Top of mind, tip of tongue
Emotion	When we care, we share
Public	Built to show, built to grow
Practical Value	News you can use
Stories	Information travels under the guise of idle chatter

So if we're trying to make a product or idea contagious, think about how to build in these key STEPPS.

Some of this can happen in the design of the product or idea itself. The hundred-dollar cheesesteak was engineered to have Social Currency. Rebecca Black's song was frequently triggered because of its title. Susan Boyle's performance evoked lots of Emotion. Movember raised millions for men's cancer by taking a once private behavior and using moustaches to make it Public.

Ken Craig's "Clean Ears Everytime" video is two minutes of pure Practical Value.

But these STEPPS can also be built into messaging around a product or idea. Blendtec's blenders had always been powerful, but by showing that power in a remarkable way, the *Will It Blend?* videos generated Social Currency and got people buzzing. Kit Kat didn't change its product, but by linking it to a popular beverage (coffee), the company increased the number of Triggers to make people think (and talk) about the candy bar. People share Vanguard's *MoneyWhys* because they provide Practical Value, but passing them along boosts word of mouth for the company itself. People shared Dove's "Evolution" video because it evokes lots of Emotion, but by embedding itself in the narrative, Dove benefits from the chatter as well.

If you want to apply this framework, here's a checklist you can use to see how well your product or idea is doing on the six different STEPPS.

Follow these six key STEPPS, or even just a few of them, and you can harness social influence and word of mouth to get any product or idea to catch on.

One last note. The best part of the STEPPS framework is that anyone can use it. It doesn't require a huge advertising budget, marketing genius, or some sort of creativity gene. Yes, the viral videos and contagious content we've talked about were created by particular individuals, but not all of them were famous or could boast ten thousand followers on Twitter. They relied on one or more of the six key STEPPS and this made their products and ideas more contagious.

Social Currency	Does talking about your product or idea make people look good? Can you find the inner remarkability? Leverage game mechanics? Make people feel like insiders?
Triggers	Consider the context. What cues make people think about your product or idea? How can you grow the habitat and make it come to mind more often?
Emotion	Focus on feelings. Does talking about your product or idea generate emotion? How can you kindle the fire?
Public	Does your product or idea advertise itself? Can people see when others are using it? If not, how can you make the private public? Can you create behavioral residue that sticks around even after people use it?
Practical Value	Does talking about your product or idea help people help others? How can you highlight incredible value, packaging your knowledge and expertise into useful information others will want to disseminate?
Stories	What is your Trojan Horse? Is your product or idea embedded in a broader narrative that people want to share? Is the story not only viral, but also valuable?

Howard Wein needed a way to help a new restaurant break through the clutter, a way to raise awareness while staying true to the Barclay Prime brand. The hundred-dollar cheesesteak did just that. It not only provided a remarkable (Social Currency), surprising (Emotion) narrative (Story) but also illustrated the type of quality product that the steakhouse offered (Practical Value). And the prevalence of cheesesteaks in Philadelphia offered ready reminders for people to pass it on (Triggers). The hundred-dollar cheesesteak got people talking and helped make Barclay Prime a rousing success.

George Wright had almost no marketing budget. He needed a way to generate buzz about a product most people wouldn't ordinarily talk about: a blender. By thinking about what made his product compelling and wrapping that idea in a broader narrative, he was able to generate hundreds of millions of views and boost sales. The *Will It Blend?* clips are amazing (Emotion) and remarkable (Social Currency). But by making the product's benefits (Practical Value) integral to a broader narrative (Stories), the videos provided a perfect Trojan horse to get people talking about an everyday household appliance and make Blendtec catch on.

Regular people with regular products and ideas. But by harnessing the psychology of word of mouth, they were able to make their products and ideas succeed.

Throughout the book we've discussed cutting-edge science about how word of mouth and social influence work. If you follow these six key STEPPS, you can make any product or idea contagious.

Acknowledgments

Whenever I said I was writing a book, people often asked whether anyone was helping me. While I did not have a co-author, that question was tough to answer because this book would never have reached fruition without countless people's help.

First, I want to thank my various collaborators over the years. People like Ezgi Akpinar, Eric Bradlow, Dave Balter and the team at BzzAgent, Gráinne Fitzsimons, Raghu Iyengar, Ed Keller and the folks at Keller Fay Group, Blake McShane, Katy Milkman, Eric Schwartz, and Morgan Ward, without whom the papers I discussed in the book would not have been possible. Bright students like Rebecca Greenblatt, Diana Jiang, Lauren McDevitt, Geneva Long, Keri Taub, and Jennifer Wu helped support these projects. Malcolm Gladwell wrote the amazing book that sent me down this road. Anna Mastri pushed me to be a better writer, and books by Seth Godin, Stanley Lieberson, Everett Rogers, Emanuel Rosen, Thomas Schelling, and Jonathan Weiner inspired me to pursue this line of research. A debt of gratitude also goes out to people like Glenn Moglen, who introduced me to academic research; Emily Pronin, who introduced me to social psychology; Noah Mark, who introduced me to sociology; and Lee Ross and Itamar Simonson, who said to always shoot for big ideas. Thanks also to all my colleagues at Wharton and Stanford and all the teachers and staff at Montgomery Blair High School and Takoma Park Middle School who taught me, and thousands of other lucky kids, about the wonders of math and science.

Second, I want to thank the people who made the book itself possible. Dan Ariely, Dan Gilbert, and Sarah Lehrer helped me understand what writing a book really meant. Alice LaPlante sharpened the writing. Jim Levine and all of his colleagues at Levine Greenberg Literary Agency were guiding lights throughout the process. Jonathan Karp, Bob Bender, Tracey Guest, Richard Rhorer, Michael Accordino, and the rest of the team at Simon & Schuster helped form these ideas into a real book. Anthony Cafaro, Colleen Chorak, Ken Craig, Ben Fischman, Denise Grady, Koreen Johannessen, Scott MacEachern, Jim Meehan, Tim Piper, Ken Segall, Brian Shebairo, Howard Wein, and George Wright took the time to share their stories with me. Various Wharton Executive EMBA students were nice enough to provide feedback on the draft. The UPenn lunchtime soccer crew provided a welcome break from writing. Maria Ana brought an eagle eye to revising. My brother, Fred, Danny, and the whole Bruno family not only gave feedback on the drafts but reminded me why I was doing all of this in the first place.

A few more people deserve special note. First, to Chip, who not only has been an advisor, mentor, and friend, but has taught me most of what I know about writing and research: I cannot thank you enough. Second, to Jordan for sticking through the process with me and being both a thoughtful editor and a tireless champion, depending on what was needed. Third, to my parents, Diane Arkin and Jeffrey Berger, not only for reading and supporting this project, but for laying the groundwork to make it all possible. And finally, to my grandmother. For kicking off this journey and supporting me along the way.

Notes

Introduction: Why Things Catch On
Page

2 *Sixty percent are gone:* www.econ.ucsb.edu/~tedb/Courses/Ec1F07/restaurantsfail.pdf.

3 *"It was like eating gold":* Taken from Barclay Prime's Yelp page, http://www.yelp.com/biz/barclay-prime-philadelphia.

4 *Most restaurants bomb:* Shane, Scott (2008), "Startup Failure Rates—The REAL numbers," *Small Business Trends*, April 28, http://smallbiztrends.com/2008/04/startup-failure-rates.html.

7 *People share more than 16,000 words:* See Mehl, Matthais R., Simine Vazire, Nairan Ramirez-Esparza, Richard B. Slatcher, and James W. Pennebaker (2007), "Are Women Really More Talkative Than Men?" *Science* 317, 82.

7 *100 million conversations about brands:* see Keller, Ed, and Barak Libai (2009), "A Holistic Approach to the Measurement of WOM," presentation at ESOMAR Worldwide Media Measurement Conference, Stockholm (May 4–6).

7 *We try websites our neighbors recommend:* see Trusov, Michael, Randolph E. Bucklin, and Koen Pauwels (2009), "Effects of Word-of-Mouth Versus Traditional Marketing: Findings from an Internet Social Networking Site," *Journal of Marketing* 73 (September), 90–102.

7 *Word of mouth is the primary factor:* Bughin, Jacques, Jonathan Doogan, and Ole Jørgen Vetvik (2010), "A New Way to Measure Word-of-Mouth Marketing," *McKinsey Quarterly* (white paper).

7 *Goel, Watts, and Goldstein 2012:* "The Structure of Online Diffusion

Networks," *Proceedings of the 13th ACM Conference on Electronic Commerce* (EC '12).

7 *$200 increase in restaurant sales:* see Godes, David, and Dina Mayzlin (2009), "Firm-Created Word-of-Mouth Communication: Evidence from a Field Study," *Marketing Science* 28, no. 4, 721–39.

8 *twenty more books sold:* Chevalier, Judith, and Dina Mayzlin (2006), "The Effect of Word of Mouth on Sales: Online Book Reviews," *Journal of Marketing Research* 43, no. 3, 345–54.

8 *Doctors are more likely:* Iyengar, Raghuram, Christophe Van den Bulte, and Thomas W. Valente (2011), "Opinion Leadership and Social Contagion in New Product Diffusion," *Marketing Science* 30, no. 2, 195–212.

8 *People are more likely:* Christakis, Nicholas A., and James Fowler (2009), *Connected: The Surprising Power of Our Social Networks and How They Shape Our Lives* (New York: Little, Brown and Company).

8 *while traditional advertising is still useful:* Stephen, Andrew, and Jeff Galak (2012), "The Effects of Traditional and Social Earned Media on Sales: A Study of a Microlending Marketplace," *Journal of Marketing Research* (forthcoming); Trusov, Bucklin, and Pauwels, "Effects of Word-of-Mouth Versus Traditional Marketing."

9 *customers referred by their friends:* Schmitt, Philipp, Bernd Skiera, and Christophe Van den Bulte (2011), "Referral Programs and Customer Value," *Journal of Marketing* 75 (January), 46–59. See also http://techcrunch.com/2011/11/27/social-proof-why-people-like -to-follow-the-crowd.

11 *Millions of people use these sites:* Eridon, Corey (2011), "25 Billion Pieces of Content Get Shared on Facebook Monthly," *Hubspot Blog,* December 2, http://blog.hubspot.com/blog/tabid/6307/bid /29407/25-Billion-Pieces-of-Content-Get-Shared-on-Facebook -Monthly-INFOGRAPHIC.aspx.

11 *The actual number is 7 percent:* This book provides a really nice perspective on the importance of face-to-face word of mouth: Keller, Ed, and Brad Fay (2012), *The Face-to-Face Book: Why Real Relationships Rule in a Digital Marketplace* (New York: Free Press).

11 *Close to two hours a day:* See http://news.cnet.com/8301-1023_3 -10421016-93.html.

12 *the average tweet:* Arthur, Charles (2009), "Average Twitter User has 126 Followers, and Only 20% of Users Go via Website," *The Guardian,* March 29, http://www.guardian.co.uk/technology/blog/2009 /jun/29/twitter-users-average-api-traffic.

12 *offline discussions are more prevalent:* When thinking about whether

online or offline word of mouth will be more effective, also think about where the desired action is taking place. If you're trying to get people to check out a website, then online word of mouth is great because the desired action is only a click away. The same thing is true with offline products or behaviors. Online word of mouth about pasta sauce is great, but people need to remember to buy it when they're actually in the store, so offline word of mouth may be even better. Also think about whether and where people do research before they buy. While most people buy a car offline, they do a lot of research online and may make their decision before they ever step into the dealership. In those instances, online word of mouth may sway their decision.

12 *Only one-third of 1 percent:* See http://articles.businessinsider.com/2009 -05-20/tech/30027787_1_tubemogul-videos-viral-hits.

13 *"by the efforts":* Gladwell, Malcolm (2000), *The Tipping Point: How Little Things Can Make a Big Difference* (New York: Little, Brown).

13 *"one in 10 Americans":* Keller, Ed, and Jon Berry (2003), *The Influentials: One American in Ten Tells the Other Nine How to Vote, Where to Eat, and What to Buy* (New York: Free Press).

14 *making things go viral:* Right now there is little good empirical evidence that people who have more social ties or who are more persuasive have a bigger impact on what catches on. See Bakshy, Eytan, Jake Hofman, Winter A. Mason, and Duncan J. Watts (2011), "Everyone's an Influencer: Quantifying Influence on Twitter," *Proceedings of the Fourth International Conference on Web Search and Data Mining*, Hong Kong; see also Watts, Duncan J., and Peter S. Dodds (2007), "Networks, Influence, and Public Opinion Formation," *Journal of Consumer Research* 34, no. 4, 441–58. Think about the last story someone told you that you passed on. Did you share it because the person who told you was really popular? Or because the story itself was so funny or surprising? Think about the last news article someone sent you that you forwarded on to someone else. Did you pass it along because the person who sent it was particularly persuasive? Or because you knew someone else would be interested in the information the story contained? In these and most other cases, the driving force behind word of mouth is the message, not the messenger.

15 *Tom Dickson was looking for a new job:* Sauer, Patrick J. (2008), "Confessions of a Viral Video Superstar," *Inc.* magazine, June 19. Go to http://jonahberger.com to see Tom blending an iPhone.

16 *in 1999 Blendtec was founded:* See http://donteattheshrimp.com

/2007/07/03/will-it-blend-gets-blendtec-in-the-wsj/ and http://
magazine.byu.edu/?act=view&a=2391 for some good discussions
of the early years at Blendtec.

1. Social Currency

Page

31 *Brian decided:* Interviews with Brian Shebairo on May 16, 2012, and
Jim Meehan on May 13, 2012.

33 *40 percent of what people talk about:* Dunbar, Robert I. M., Anna
Marriott, and N. D. C. Duncan (1997), "Human Conversational
Behavior," *Human Nature* 8, no. 3, 231–44.

33 *half of tweets are "me" focused:* Naaman, Mor, Jeffrey Boase, and Chih-
Hui Lai (2010), "Is It Really About Me? Message Content in Social
Awareness Streams," *Proceedings of the ACM Conference*, 189–92.

33 *Jason Mitchell and Diana Tamir:* Tamir, Diana I., and Jason P.
Mitchell (2012), "Disclosing Information About the Self Is Intrinsically Rewarding," *Proceedings of the National Academy of Sciences* 109,
no. 21, 8038–43.

36 *We make educated guesses:* See Berger, Jonah, and Chip Heath (2008),
"Who Drives Divergence? Identity Signaling, Outgroup Dissimi-
larity, and the Abandonment of Cultural Tastes," *Journal of Personality and Social Psychology* 95, no. 3, 593–605. See also Berger, Jonah,
and Chip Heath (2007), "Where Consumers Diverge from Others:
Identity Signaling and Product Domains," *Journal of Consumer Research* 34, no. 2, 121–34, for discussions of research in this area.

36 *Prada handbag:* Wojnicki, Andrea C., and Dave Godes (2010),
"Word-of-Mouth as Self-Enhancement," University of Toronto
working paper. See also De Angelis, Matteo, Andrea Bonezzi,
Alessandro Peluso, Derek Rucker, and Michele Costabile (2012),
"On Braggarts and Gossips: A Self-Enhancement Account of
Word-of-Mouth Generation and Transmission," *Journal of Market-
ing Research,* forthcoming.

38 *Something "out of the ordinary":* For a discussion of the story behind Snapple facts, see http://mittelmitte.blogspot.com/2006/09
/snapple-real-facts-are-100-true.html and http://mysnapplerealfacts
.blogspot.com/.

39 *Wharton professor Raghu Iyengar:* Berger, Jonah, and Raghuram Iyengar (2013), "How Interest Shapes Word-of-Mouth over Different
Channels," Wharton working paper.

40 *More interesting tweets:* Bakshy, Eytan, Jake M. Hofman, Winter A.
Mason, and Duncan J. Watts (2011), "Everyone's an Influencer:

Quantifying Influence on Twitter," *WSDM,* 65–74. See also Berger, Jonah, and Katherine Milkman (2012), "What Makes Online Content Viral," *Journal of Marketing Research* 49, no. 2, 192–205.

40 *psychologists from the University of Illinois:* Burrus, Jeremy, Justin Kruger, and Amber Jurgens (2006), "The Truth Never Stands in the Way of a Good Story: The Distortion of Stories in the Service of Entertainment," University of Illinois working paper.

42 *One way to generate surprise:* Heath, Chip, and Dan Heath (2011), *Made to Stick: Why Some Ideas Survive and Others Die* (New York: Random House).

42 *Mysteries and controversy:* Ibid. See also Chen, Zoey, and Jonah Berger (2012), "When, Why, and How Controversy Causes Conversation," Wharton working paper.

43 *Shot on a handheld camera:* Details about *The Blair Witch Project* can be found at http://en.wikipedia.org/wiki/The_Blair_Witch_Project.

43 *black toilet paper:* Information about Renova, the Portuguese company that makes colored toilet paper, can be found at http://www.renovaonline.net/_global/.

45 *180 million people:* The facts about frequent flier programs came from http://www.frequentflyerservices.com/press_room/facts_and_stats/frequent_flyer_facts.php and http://www.prweb.com/releases/2011/11/prweb8925371.htm.

46 *discrete markers motivate us:* Information about how goals can act as reference points and how discrete progress markers can affect motivation can be found in: Heath, Chip, Richard P. Larrick, and George Wu (1999), "Goals as Reference Points," *Cognitive Psychology* 38, 79–109; Amir, On, and Dan Ariely (2008), "Resting on Laurels: The Effects of Discrete Progress Markers as Sub-goals on Task Performance and Preferences," *Journal of Experimental Psychology: Learning, Memory, and Cognition* 34, no. 5, 1158–71; and Kivetz, Ran, Oleg Urminsky, and Yuhuang Zheng (2006), "The Goal-Gradient Hypothesis Resurrected: Purchase Acceleration, Illusionary Goal Progress, and Customer Retention," *Journal of Marketing Research* 43, no. 1, 39–56.

46 *By increasing motivation, the cards:* Kivetz, Ran, Oleg Urminsky, and Yuhuang Zheng (2006), "The Goal-Gradient Hypothesis Resurrected: Purchase Acceleration, Illusionary Goal Progress, and Customer Retention," *Journal of Marketing Research,* 43 (February), 39–58.

47 *They preferred to do better:* Solnick, S. J., and D. Hemenway (1998), "Is More Always Better? A Survey on Positional Concerns." *Journal of Economic Behavior and Organization* 37, 373–83.

50 *the contest helped drive sales:* Information about Burberry's "Art of the Trench" campaign can be found at http://blogs.wsj.com/source /2010/01/19/burberry%E2%80%99s-trench-website-too-good -to-be-true/ and http://www.1to1media.com/weblog/2010/01/internet _marketing_from_the_tr.html.

53 *"It's like the concierge":* Interview with Ben Fischman on June 12, 2012. Thanks to Dave Balter for introducing me to this great story.

54 *If something is difficult to obtain:* For a discussion of how effort influences inferences of value, see Aronson, Elliot (1997), "The Theory of Cognitive Dissonance: The Evolution and Vicissitudes of an Idea," in *The Message of Social Psychology: Perspectives on Mind in Society,* ed. Craig McGarty and S. Alexander Haslam (Malden, Mass.: Blackwell Publishing), 20–35; and Aronson, Elliot, and Judson Mills (1959), "The Effect of Severity of Initiation on Liking for a Group," *Journal of Abnormal and Social Psychology* 66, no. 6, 584–88. See also Sela, Aner, and Jonah Berger (2011), "Decision Quicksand: How Trivial Choices Suck Us In," *Journal of Consumer Research,* 39.

54 *People evaluate cookbooks:* There are a number of valuable papers on how scarcity affects value. See Verhallen, Theo (1982), "Scarcity and Consumer Choice Behavior," *Journal of Economic Psychology* 2, 299–322; Worchel, S., J. Lee, and A. Adewole (1975), "Effects of Supply and Demand on Ratings of Object Value," *Journal of Personality and Social Psychology* 32, 906–14; Fromkin, H. L., J. C. Olson, R. L. Dipboye, and D. Barnaby (1971), "A Commodity Theory Analysis of Consumer Preferences for Scarce Products," *Proceedings 79th Annual Convention of the American Psychological Association,* 1971, pp. 653–54.

56 *Chicken McNuggets:* Thanks to Dave Balter for telling me about the McRib locator. For background details on the story, see http:// www.maxim.com/funny/the-cult-of-the-mcrib-0 and http://en .wikipedia.org/wiki/McRib.

59 *as soon as you pay people:* For early (and extremely clever) research on intrinsic and extrinsic motivation, see Lepper, Mark R., David Greene, and Richard E. Nisbett (1973), "Undermining Children's Intrinsic Interest with Extrinsic Reward: A Test of the 'Overjustification' Hypothesis," *Journal of Social and Personality Psychology* 28, no. 1, 129–37. For a more recent treatment, see Heyman, James, and Dan Ariely (2004), "Effort for Payment: A Tale of Two Markets," *Psychological Science* 15, no. 11, 787–93.

2. Triggers

62 *"Nobody talks about boring companies":* Sernovitz, Andy (2006), *Word of Mouth Marketing: How Smart Companies Get People Talking* (Chicago: Kaplan Publishing).

62 *People talk about Cheerios:* The finding that Honey Nut Cheerios get more word of mouth than Walt Disney World comes from the BzzAgent analysis we discuss in this chapter: Berger, Jonah, and Eric Schwartz (2011), "What Drives Immediate and Ongoing Word-of-Mouth?" *Journal of Marketing,* October, 869–80. The finding also comes from Twitter data on the frequency with which these two brands are discussed.

64 *sixteen word-of-mouth episodes:* Carl, Walter (2006), "What's All the Buzz About? Everyday Communication and the Relational Basis of Word-of-Mouth and Buzz Marketing Practices," *Management Communication Quarterly* 19, 601–34.

64 *American consumers mention specific brands:* Keller, Ed, and Barak Libai (2009), "A Holistic Approach to the Measurement of WOM," presentation at ESOMAR Worldwide Media Measurement Conference, Stockholm (May 4–6).

66 *Dave gave my colleague Eric Schwartz:* This included information about the product in each campaign and the number of BzzReports each BzzAgent submitted. We were especially interested in the fact that we could analyze the buzz generated by each product by agent. After all, certain people might share more word of mouth than others: Chatty Cathys talk more than Quiet Quentins. But by looking at how much individual agents talked across different campaigns, we could identify patterns. We could see whether an agent talked more about a coffee brand than a new type of digital camera. And we could start to understand why certain products got more word of mouth than others. Not just whether people talked about certain product categories (such as food) more than others (such as movies), but what really drives discussion in the first place—the psychology of talk.

69 *some thoughts are more top of mind:* Accessibility is a huge topic in psychology; for some classic research on the topic, see Higgins, E. Tory, and G. King (1981), "Accessibility of Social Constructs: Information-processing Consequences of Individual and Contextual Variability," in *Personality, Cognition, and Social Interaction,* ed. N. Cantor and J. F. Kihlstrom (Hillsdale, N.J.: Lawrence Erlbaum),

60–81; and Wyer, Robert S., and T. K. Srull (1981), "Category Accessibility: Some Theoretical and Empirical Issues Concerning the Processing of Social Stimulus Information," in *Social Cognition: The Ontario Symposium,* vol. 1, ed. E. T. Higgins, C. P. Herman, and M. P. Zanna (Hillsdale, N. J.: Lawrence Erlbaum), 161–97.

69 *Some things are chronically accessible:* For an early paper on chronic accessibility, see Bargh, John A., W. J. Lombardi, and E. Tory Higgins (1988), "Automaticity of Chronically Accessible Constructs in Person X Situation Effects on Person Perception: It's Just a Matter of Time," *Journal of Personality and Social Psychology* 55, no. 4, 599–605.

70 *stimuli in the surrounding environment:* There is a huge literature on stimuli in the environment and spreading activation, but for some classics, see Anderson, John R. (1983), *The Architecture of Cognition* (Cambridge, Mass.: Harvard University Press); Collins, Allan M., and Elizabeth F. Loftus (1975), "A Spreading-Activation Theory of Semantic Processing," *Psychological Review* 82, no. 6, 407–28; and Higgins, Tory E., William S. Rholes, and Carl R. Jones (1977), "Category Accessibility and Impression Formation," *Journal of Social Psychology* 13 (March), 141–54. For examples in a consumption context, see Nedungadi, P. (1990), "Recall and Consumer Consideration Sets: Influencing Choice Without Altering Brand Evaluations," *Journal of Consumer Research* 17, no. 3, 263–76; and Berger, Jonah, and Gráinne M. Fitzsimons (2008), "Dogs on the Street, Pumas on Your Feet: How Cues in the Environment Influence Product Evaluation and Choice," *Journal of Marketing Research* 45, no. 1, 1–14.

70 *the candy company Mars:* White, Michael (1997), "Toy Rover Sales Soar into Orbit: Mars Landing Puts Gold Shine Back into Space Items," *Arizona Republic,* July 12A, E1.

71 *Music researchers Adrian North:* North, Adrian C., David J. Hargreaves, and Jennifer McKendrick (1997), "In-Store Music Affects Product Choice," *Nature* 390 (November), 132.

71 *Psychologist Gráinne Fitzsimons:* Berger and Fitzsimons, "Dogs on the Street," 1–14.

73 *people possess core beliefs:* Riker, William, and Peter Ordeshook (1968), "A Theory of the Calculus of Voting," *American Political Science Review* 62, no. 1, 25–42.

74 *Arizona's 2000 general election:* Berger, Jonah, Marc Meredith, and S. Christian Wheeler (2008), "Contextual Priming: Where People Vote Affects How They Vote," *Proceedings of the National Academy of Sciences* 105, no. 26, 8846–49.

76 *Rebecca's parents paid four thousand dollars:* Details about Rebecca Black came from http://en.wikipedia.org/wiki/Rebecca_Black.

78 *Triggers boost word of mouth:* Also see Rosen, Emanuel (2003), *Anatomy of Buzz* (London: Profile Books), for a nice related discussion of triggers.

78 *More frequently triggered products:* Berger, Jonah, and Eric Schwartz (2011), "What Drives Immediate and Ongoing Word-of-Mouth?" *Journal of Marketing,* October, 869–80.

80 *analyzed hundreds of* New York Times *book reviews:* Berger, Jonah, Alan T. Sorensen, and Scott J. Rasmussen (2010), "Positive Effects of Negative Publicity: When Negative Reviews Increase Sales," *Marketing Science* 29, no. 5, 815–27.

81 *the Kit Kat tune:* Details about Kit Kat's history came from http://en.wikipedia.org/wiki/Kit_Kat. Details about the coffee campaign came from an interview with Colleen Chorak on February 9, 2012.

81 *one of the top ten "earworms":* Details about the "Give me a Break" song being an earworm came from Kellaris, James (2003), "Dissecting Earworms: Further Evidence on the 'Song-Stuck-in-Your Head' Phenomenon," presentation to the Society for Consumer Psychology. See also http://www.webmd.com/mental-health/news/20030227/songs-stick-in-everyones-head.

83 *ideas also have habitats:* Berger, Jonah, and Chip Heath (2005), "Idea Habitats: How the Prevalence of Environmental Cues Influences the Success of Ideas," *Cognitive Science* 29, no. 2, 195–221.

84 *an experiment we conducted with BzzAgent and Boston Market:* Berger and Schwartz, "What Drives Immediate and Ongoing Word-of-Mouth?" 869–80.

85 *"Bob, I've got emphysema":* See http://no-smoke.org/images/02_Bob_14x48.jpg.

85 *the poison parasite:* Cialdini, Robert B., Petia Petrova, Linda Demaine, Daniel Barrett, Brad Sagarin, Jon Manner, and Kelton Rhoads (2005), "The Poison Parasite Defense: A Strategy for Sapping a Stronger Opponent's Persuasive Strength," University of Arizona working paper.

86 *Anheuser-Busch revised the slogan:* Cialdini, Robert B. (2001), *Influence: Science and Practice* (Needham Heights, Mass.: Allyn & Bacon).

86 *Poke too many holes:* Information about the fan effect can be found in Anderson, John R. (1974), "Retrieval of Propositional Information from Long-term Memory," *Cognitive Psychology* 6, 451–74; and Anderson, John R. (1983), *The Architecture of Cognition* (Cambridge, Mass.: Harvard University Press).

87 *out spills fat:* To see the Department of Health's campaign in action, visit http://jonahberger.com.

89 *products associated with the color orange:* Berger and Fitzsimons, "Dogs on the Street," 1–14.

90 *you'll notice a neat pattern:* Thanks to Scott A. Golder for providing these data.

3. Emotion

Page

93 *schlieren photography:* Grady's article about the cough can be found at Grady, Denise (2008), "The Mysterious Cough, Caught on Film," *New York Times,* October 27; http://www.nytimes.com/2008/10/28 /science/28cough.html. The *New England Journal of Medicine* article on which her piece is based is Tang, Julian W., and Gary S. Settles (2008), "Coughing and Aerosols," *New England Journal of Medicine* 359, 15.

100 *That doesn't really tell us much:* Not surprisingly, external factors like where an article was featured also correlated with whether an article made the list. Articles that appeared on the front page of the physical newspaper were shared more than those placed inside. Articles featured at the top of the *Times* home page were shared more than those buried several clicks into the website. Articles written by U2's Bono or former senator Bob Dole were shared more often than articles written by less famous authors. But these relationships are neither that surprising nor that helpful. Buying a Super Bowl ad or hiring Bono will help increase the chance that content gets viewed and shared. Most people, however, don't have the funding or personal connections to make those things happen. Instead, we focused on aspects of the content itself that were linked to sharing.

101 *More useful articles:* A full description of our research on *The New York Times* Most E-Mailed list, as well as our findings, can be found in Berger, Jonah, and Katherine Milkman (2012), "What Makes Online Content Viral," *Journal of Marketing Research* 49, no. 2, 192–205.

102 *awe is the sense of wonder:* For a great overview article on awe, see Keltner, D., and J. Haidt (2003), "Approaching Awe, a Moral, Spiritual, and Aesthetic Emotion," *Cognition and Emotion*, 17, 297–314. For a more recent empirical treatment, see Shiota, M. N., D. Keltner, and A. Mossman (2007), "The Nature of Awe: Elicitors, Appraisals, and Effects on Self-concept," *Cognition and Emotion* 21, 944–63.

102 *"The most beautiful emotion":* The Einstein quote comes from Ulam, S. M., Françoise Ulam, and Jan Myielski (1976), *Adventures of a Mathematician* (New York: Charles Scribner's Sons), 289.

103 *Awe-inspiring articles:* Berger and Milkman, "What Makes Online Content Viral," 192–205.

104 *Susan Boyle's first appearance:* Susan Boyle's performance can be found at http://jonahberger.com.

105 *helps deepen our social connection:* For a discussion of how the social sharing of emotion deepens social bonds, see Peters, Kim, and Yoshihasa Kashima (2007), "From Social Talk to Social Action: Shaping the Social Triad with Emotion Sharing," *Journal of Personality and Social Psychology* 93, no. 5, 780–97.

106 *negative content should be more viral:* For a discussion of positive and negative word of mouth, see Godes, Dave, Yubo Chen, Sanjiv Das, Chrysanthos Dellarocas, Bruce Pfeiffer, et al. (2005), "The Firm's Management of Social Interactions," *Marketing Letters* 16, nos. 3–4, 415–28.

106 *psychologist Jamie Pennebaker:* A discussion of linguistic inquiry and word count can be found in: Pennebaker, James W., Roger J. Booth, and Martha E. Francis (2007), "Linguistic Inquiry and Word Count: LIWC2007," accessed October 14, 2011; http://www.liwc.net/. For a review of how LIWC has been used to study a range of psychological processes, see Pennebaker, James W., Matthias R. Mehl, and Katie Niederhoffer (2003), "Psychological Aspects of Natural Language Use: Our Words, Our Selves," *Annual Review of Psychology* 54, 547–77.

106 *the amount of positivity and negativity:* The greater the percentage of emotional words in a passage of text, the more emotion it tends to express. Pennebaker, J. W., and M. E. Francis (1996), "Cognitive, Emotional, and Language Processes in Disclosure," *Cognition and Emotion* 10, 601–26.

107 *newcomers falling in love with New York City:* Berger and Milkman, "What Makes Online Content Viral," 192–205.

108 *Articles that evoked anger or anxiety:* Ibid.

108 *physiological arousal:* A great deal of research in psychology has examined the so-called two-dimensional theory of affect (valence and arousal). For discussions, see Barrett, Lisa Feldman, and James A. Russell (1999), "The Structure of Current Affect: Controversies and Emerging Consensus," *Current Directions in Psychological Science* 8, no. 1, 10–14; Christie, I. C., and B. H. Friedman (2004), "Autonomic Specificity of Discrete Emotion and Dimensions of

Affective Space: A Multivariate Approach," *International Journal of Psychophysiology* 51, 143–53; and Schlosberg, H. (1954), "Three Dimensions of Emotion," *Psychological Review* 61, no. 2, 81–88.

108　*This is arousal:* For a discussion of the neurobiology of arousal, see Heilman, K. M. (1997), "The Neurobiology of Emotional Experience," *Journal of Neuropsychiatry* 9, 439–48.

110　*funny content is shared:* The result that arousal boosts social transmission can be found in Berger, Jonah (2011), "Arousal Increases Social Transmission of Information," *Psychological Science* 22, no. 7, 891–93.

111　*While traveling to a gig:* A summary of Dave Carroll's odyssey with United Airlines can be found in his book: Carroll, Dave (2012), *United Breaks Guitars: The Power of One Voice in the Age of Social Media* (Carlsbad, CA: Hay House). To hear the actual song, go to http://jonahberger.com.

115　*The clip tells a budding love story:* A clip of "Parisian Love" can be viewed at http://jonahberger.com. The story behind "Parisian Love" came from an interview with Anthony Cafaro on June 20, 2012.

116　*"The best results don't show up in a search engine":* The quote came from Iezzi, Teressa (2010), "Meet the Google Five," http://creativity -online.com/news/the-google-creative-lab/146084.

117　*Simply adding more arousal:* Berger and Milkman, "What Makes Online Content Viral," 192–205.

117　*obesity reduces life expectancy:* The statistic about obesity came from Whitlock, Gary, Sarah Lewington, Paul Sherliker, and Richard Peto (2009), "Body-mass Index and Mortality," *The Lancet* 374, no. 9684, 114.

118　*disgust is a highly arousing emotion:* For a discussion of how disgust affects social transmission, see Heath, Chip, Chris Bell, and Emily Sternberg (2001), "Emotional Selection in Memes: The Case of Urban Legends," *Journal of Personality and Social Psychology* 81, no. 6, 1028–41.

118　*the practice strengthens the maternal bond:* To learn more about baby-wearing and attachment, see www.attachmentparenting.org.

118　*the company created an ad centered on the aches:* To see a clip of the Motrin ad, see http://jonahberger.com.

119　*the marketing debacle:* Learmonth, Michael (2008), "How Twittering Critics Brought Down Motrin Mom Campaign: Bloggers Ignite Brush Fire over Weekend, Forcing J&J to Pull Ads, Issue Apology," *AdAge.com,* November 17, retrieved from http://adage

.com/article/digital/twittering-critics-brought-motrin-mom
-campaign/132622.

4. Public

Page

125 *Ken Segall was Steve Jobs's right hand man:* All taken from my interview with Ken Segall on May, 15, 2012. For more information on
Ken's work with Apple, see Segall (2012), *Insanely Simple: The Ob-
session That Drives Apple's Success* (New York: Portfolio/Penguin).

128 *If lots of people are eating there:* For an economist's take on this issue,
see Becker, Gary S. (1991), "A Note on Restaurant Pricing and
Other Examples of Social Influence on Price," *Journal of Political
Economy* 99, no. 3, 1109–16.

128 *pick entrées preferred by other diners:* For evidence of social influence
in entrée choice, see Cai, Hongbi, Yuyu Chen, and Hanming Fang
(2009), "Observational Learning: Evidence from a Randomized
Natural Field Experiment," *American Economic Review* 99, no. 3,
864–82. For research on conformity in hotel towel use, see Goldstein, Noah J., Robert B. Cialdini, and Vladas Griskevicius (2008),
"A Room with a Viewpoint: Using Social Norms to Motivate
Environmental Conservation in Hotels," *Journal of Consumer Research* 35, 472–82. Similar approaches have also been applied to get
people to reduce home energy consumption.

128 *People are more likely to vote:* For evidence of social influence in voter
turnout, see Nickerson, David W. (2008), "Is Voting Contagious?
Evidence from Two Field Experiments," *American Political Science
Review* 102, 49–57. For a discussion of how social influence may
affect obesity and smoking cessation, see Christakis, Nicholas A.,
and James Fowler (2009), *Connected: The Surprising Power of Our
Social Networks and How They Shape Our Lives* (New York: Little,
Brown, and Company).

128 *what brand of coffee to buy:* For evidence of social influence in coffee
choice, see Burnkrant, Robert E., and Alain Cousineau (1975), "Informational and Normative Social Influence in Buyer Behavior,"
Journal of Consumer Research 2, 206–15. For evidence of social influence in paying taxes, see Thaler, Richard (2012), "Watching Behavior Before Writing the Rules," *New York Times,* July 12, retrieved
from http://www.nytimes.com/2012/07/08/business/behavioral-sci
ence-can-help-guide-policy-economic-view.html.

128 *people are more likely to laugh:* For evidence about social influence in
laughter, see Provine, R. R. (1992), "Contagious Laughter: Laughter

Is a Sufficient Stimulus for Laughs and Smiles," *Bulletin of the Psychonomic Society* 30, 1–4.

128 *"social proof":* Cialdini, Robert B. (2001), *Influence: Science and Practice* (Needham Heights, Mass.: Allyn & Bacon).

130 *when she looked at hundreds of kidney donations:* The findings from Juanjuan's clever paper, as well as assorted statistics about kidney failure and donation, can be found at Zhang, Juanjuan (2010), "The Sound of Silence: Observational Learning in the U.S. Kidney Market," *Marketing Science* 29, no. 2, 315–35.

132 *Koreen Johannessen started:* Interview with Koreen Johannessen on June 21, 2012.

132 *college students . . . report drinking alcohol:* For some statistics about college students' binge drinking, see Weschler, Henry, and Toben F. Nelson (2008), "What We Have Learned from the Harvard School of Public Health College Alcohol Study: Focusing Attention on College Student Alcohol Consumption and the Environmental Conditions That Promote It," *Journal of Studies on Alcohol and Drugs* 69, 481–90. Also see Hingson, Ralph, Timothy Heeren, Michael Winter, and Henry Wechsler (2005), "Magnitude of Alcohol-Related Mortality and Morbidity Among U.S. College Students Ages 18–24: Changes from 1998 to 2001," *Annual Review of Public Health*, 26, 259–79, and http://www.alcohol101plus.org/downloads/collegestudents.pdf.

133 *how they felt about drinking:* Psychologists use the term "pluralistic ignorance" to talk about this issue. Pluralistic ignorance refers to a case where most people in a group privately reject a norm (such as drinking a lot) but incorrectly assume that others accept it, in part because they can see others' behavior but not their thoughts. For a broader discussion, see Prentice, Deborah A., and Dale T. Miller (1993), "Pluralistic Ignorance and Alcohol Use on Campus: Some Consequences of Misperceiving the Social Norm," *Journal of Personality and Social Psychology* 64, no. 2, 243–56.

135 *A restaurant might be extremely popular:* This is why the maître d' will often seat the first few arrivals near the window at the front of the restaurant. As a funny side note, there is a place in New York City that I always assumed was extremely popular because it has benches outside that were always full. I assumed that the people sitting on them were waiting to eat. Only later did I realize that they may have been sitting there because it was a convenient place to rest for a few minutes.

135 *1.5 million car sales:* For the full story on our automobile research,

see McShane, Blakely, Eric T. Bradlow, and Jonah Berger (2012), "Visual Influence and Social Groups," *Journal of Marketing Research*, (forthcoming). Also see Grinblatt, M., M. Keloharrju, and S. Ikaheimo (2008), "Social Influence and Consumption: Evidence from the Automobile Purchases of Neighbors," *The Review of Economics and Statistics* 90, no. 4, 735–53.

136 *The easier something is to see:* For evidence about how public visibility affects word of mouth, see Berger, Jonah, and Eric Schwartz (2011), "What Drives Immediate and Ongoing Word of Mouth?" *Journal of Marketing Research* 48, no. 5, 869–80.

137 *cancer claims the lives:* For statistics about how cancer affects men, see http://www.cdc.gov/features/cancerandmen/ and http://www.wcrf.org/cancer_statistics/world_cancer_statistics.php.

137 *It all started one Sunday afternoon:* For the backstory on the founding of Movember, as well as statistics on its growth and development, see ca.movember.com and http://billabout.com/get-your-mo-on%E2%80%A8interview-adam-garone-movember-founder/.

140 *Johannessen was able to decrease heavy drinking:* For a related discussion, see Schroeder, Christine M., and Deborah A. Prentice (1998), "Exposing Pluralistic Ignorance to Reduce Alcohol Use Among College Students," *Journal of Applied Social Psychology* 28, 2150–80.

141 *350 million users:* For basic details and statistics about Hotmail, see http://en.wikipedia.org/wiki/Hotmail.

143 *Apple's white headphone cords stood out:* Such visible signals are particularly important in domains where there are network effects, or where the value of a product depends on the number of others who are using it.

144 *it's called* behavioral residue: The term "behavioral residue" comes from psychologist Sam Gosling. For a discussion of his research in the area, see Gosling, Sam (2008), *Snoop: What Your Stuff Says About You* (New York: Basic Books).

146 *"a stupid idea":* Mickle, Tripp (2009), "Five Strong Years," *Sports Business Daily*, September 14, retrieved from http://www.sportsbusinessdaily.com/Journal/Issues/2009/09/20090914/This-Weeks-News/Five-Strong-Years.aspx.

146 *Even Armstrong was incredulous:* Carr, Austin (2011), "Lance Armstrong, Doug Ulman Thought the Livestrong Wristband Would Fail," *Fast Company,* November 11, retrieved from http://www.fastcompany.com/article/doug-ulman-didnt-think-the-livestrong-bracelets-would-sell.

146 *This public visibility:* Many things contributed to making Livestrong

bands a success. They cost only a dollar, making it easy for people to try out being part of the movement, even if they weren't sure they wanted to commit themselves. The wristbands were also really easy to wear. Unlike breast cancer ribbons, which you have to pin on different pieces of clothing, Livestrong bands could be worn all the time. You could wear one all day, keep it on while sleeping, even wear it in the shower. You never had to take it off or remember where you left it. But color also played an important role, as discussed.

147 *"The nice thing about a wristband":* Interview with Scott MacEachern, 2006.

149 *installing these buttons:* Gelles, David (2010), "E-commerce Takes an Instant Liking to Facebook Button," *Financial Times,* September 21, retrieved from http://www.ft.com/cms/s/2/1599be2e-c5a9-11df -ab48-00144feab49a.html.

150 *whether anti-drug ads were actually effective:* Hornik, Robert, Lela Jacobsohn, Robert Orwin, Andrea Piesse, and Graham Kalton (2008), "Effects of the National Youth Anti-Drug Media Campaign on Youths," *American Journal of Public Health* 98, no. 12, 2229–36.

152 *"30 billion songs were illegally downloaded":* Recording Industry Association of America website, http://www.riaa.com/faq.php, retrieved June 1, 2012.

152 *people who stole petrified wood:* Cialdini, Robert B., Linda J. Demaine, Brad J. Sagarin, Daniel W. Barrett, Kelton Rhoads, and Patricia L. Winter (2006), "Managing Social Norms for Persuasive Impact," *Social Influence* 1, no. 1, 3–15.

5. Practical Value
Page

155 *If you had to pick someone:* Interview with Ken Craig, February 20, 2012. A clip of Ken's corn trick can be seen at http://jonahberger .com.

163 *Kahneman received the Nobel:* For a popular treatment of prospect theory, see Kahneman's book *Thinking, Fast and Slow* (2011), from Farrar, Straus and Giroux. For a more academic treatment, see Kahneman, Daniel, and Amos Tversky (1979), "Prospect Theory: An Analysis of Decision Under Risk," *Econometrica* 47 (1979), 263–91. Many of the scenarios discussed in this chapter are adapted from Richard Thaler's work on mental accounting. See Thaler, Richard (1980), "Toward a Positive Theory of Consumer Choice," *Journal of Economic Behavior and Organization* 1, 39–60;

and Thaler, Richard (1985), "Mental Accounting and Consumer Choice," *Marketing Science* 4, 199–214.

166 *To test this possibility:* Anderson and Simester's research can be found at Anderson, Eric T., and Duncan I. Simester (2001), "Are Sale Signs Less Effective When More Products Have Them?" *Marketing Science* 20, no. 2, 121–42.

166 *buy a new clock radio:* Adapted from Thaler, "Toward a Positive Theory of Consumer Choice," 39–60.

169 *While noting something is on sale:* A good deal of research has examined how saying something is on sale affects perceived value. For examples, see Blattberg, Robert, Richard A. Briesch, and Edward J. Fox (1995), "How Promotions Work," *Marketing Science* 14, no. 3, 122–32; Lattin, James M., and Randolph E. Bucklin (1989), "Reference Effects of Price and Promotion on Brand Choice Behavior," *Journal of Marketing Research* 26, no. 3, 299–310; and Raju, Jagmohan S. (1992), "The Effect of Price Promotions on Variability in Product Category Sales," *Marketing Science* 11, no. 3, 207–20. For an empirical investigation of how sale signs affect purchase, see Anderson and Simester, "Are Sale Signs Less Effective," 121–42.

169 *quantity purchase limits increase sales:* Inman, Jeffrey J., Anil C. Peter, and Priya Raghubir (1997), "Framing the Deal: The Role of Restrictions in Accentuating the Deal Value," *Journal of Consumer Research* 24 (June), 68–79.

170 *This increases Practical Value:* For evidence on how restrictions on who can get access to a deal affect perceived value, see Schindler, Robert M. (1998), "Consequences of Perceiving Oneself as Responsible for Obtaining a Discount: Evidence for Smart-Shopper Feelings," *Journal of Consumer Psychology* 7, no. 4, 371–92.

170 *whether a discount seems larger:* For evidence that perceived value is affected by absolute and relative discounts, see Chen, S.-F. S., K.B. Monroe, and Yung-Chein Lou (1998), "The Effects of Framing Price Promotion Messages on Consumers' Perceptions and Purchase Intentions," *Journal of Retailing* 74, no. 3, 353–72.

176 *You may have heard:* See the following for a discussion of the link between vaccines and autism and the consequences of the false information: McIntyre, Peter, and Julie Leask (2008), "Improving Uptake of MMR Vaccine," *British Medical Journal* 336, no. 7647, 729–30; Pepys, Mark B. (2007), "Science and Serendipity," *Clinical Medicine* 7, no. 6, 562–78; and Mnookin, Seth (2011), *The Panic Virus* (New York: Simon and Schuster).

6. Stories
Page

180 *battle took place around 1170 BC:* Estimates of the timing of the Trojan Horse come from this paper: Baikouzis, Constantino, and Marcelo O. Magnasco (2008), "Is an Eclipse Described in *The Odyssey*?" *Proceedings of the National Academy of Sciences* 105, no. 26, 8823–28.

186 *Stories . . . help us make sense of the world:* Baumeister, Roy F., Liquing Zhang, and Kathleen D. Vohs (2004), "Gossip as Cultural Learning," *Review of General Psychology* 8, 111–21.

187 *we're much more likely to be persuaded:* For research related to how stories can make it harder to counterargue, see Kardes, Frank R. (1993), "Consumer Inference: Determinants, Consequences, and Implications for Advertising," in *Advertising Exposure, Memory and Choice,* ed. Andrew A. Mitchell (Hillsdale, N.J.: Erlbaum), 163–91.

188 *He lost all that weight:* See http://en.wikipedia.org/wiki/Jared_Fogle for an overview of the Jared story.

190 *So he created a short film:* The backstory came from an interview with Tim Piper on June 18, 2012. The "Evolution" video can be seen at http://jonahberger.com.

191 *2 percent of women describe themselves as beautiful:* This fact comes from Etcoff, Nancy, Susie Orbach, Jennifer Scott, and Heidi D'Agostino (2004), *The Real Truth About Beauty: A Global Report;* retrieved on June 1, 2012, from http://www.scribd.com/doc/16653666/1/%E2%80%9CTHE-REAL-TRUTH-ABOUT-BEAUTY-A-GLOBAL-REPORT%E2%80%9D.

192 *double-digit sales growth:* See http://www.marketingvox.com/dove_evolution_goes_viral_with_triple_the_traffic_of_super_bowl_spot-022944/ retrieved on May 15, 2012. Also see http://en.wikipedia.org/wiki/Evolution_%28advertisement%29.

193 *Canadian Ron Bensimhon:* http://news.bbc.co.uk/2/hi/europe/3579148.stm.

194 *part of a publicity stunt:* For a brief discussion of the events, see BBC News (2004), "Jail Sentence for Tutu Prankster," August 19.

196 *most viewed online advertisement in history:* World Records Academy (2011), "Most Viewed Online Ad: 'Evian Roller Babies' Sets World Record," retrieved May 2012 from http://www.worldrecordsacademy.org.

196 *sales dropped almost 25 percent:* O'Leary, Noreen (2010), "Does Viral Pay?" retrieved May 21, 2011, from http://www.adweek.com.

197 *In one spot a father is grocery shopping:* To watch the Panda clip, go to http://jonahberger.com.

198 *without talking about a blender:* For further discussion of valuable virality, see Akpinar, Ezgi, and Jonah Berger (2012), "Valuable Virality," Wharton working paper.

199 *Psychologists Gordon Allport and Joseph Postman:* Allport, Gordon, and Joseph Postman (1947), *Psychology of Rumor* (New York: H. Holt and Company).

Epilogue

Page

203 *when Thuan Le arrived:* For the story of Thuan Le and the Vietnamese nail salons, see Tran, My-Thuan (2008), "A Mix of Luck, Polish," *Los Angeles Times,* May 5. Also see http://www.cnn.com/video/?/video/us/2011/07/05/pkg.wynter.vietnamese.nail.salon.cnn.

205 *Cambodian Americans own:* Ardey, Julie (2008), "Cambodian Settlers Glaze a Donut Trail," *Daily Yonder,* February 18; retrieved from http://www.dailyyonder.com/cambodian-settlers-glaze-donut-trail/2008/02/18/1062.

205 *Koreans own:* Bleyer, Jennifer (2008), "Dry Cleaners Feel an Ill Wind from China," *New York Times,* April 27.

205 *60 percent of the liquor stores in Boston:* Retrieved on March 10, 2012, from http://www.pbs.org/wgbh/amex/murder/peopleevents/p_immigrants.html.

205 *Jews produced:* Klinger, Jerry, "The Russians Are Coming, The Russians Are Coming," *America Jewish History 1880–1924*, retrieved on March 15, 2012, from http://www.jewishmag.com/85mag/usa8/usa8.htm.

206 *Duncan Watts makes a nice comparison:* Watts, Duncan J. (2007), "Challenging the Influentials Hypothesis," *WOMMA Measuring Word of Mouth* 3, 207.

Index

A

ABC News, 149
Abercrombie & Fitch, 142
Ad Age, 119
Advertising, 2, 4–7, 16, 19, 32, 125,
    187, 208
  emotions evoked by, 117, 123
  infomercials, 164–65
  misleading, as Trojan horse,
    190–91
  self, through public visibility,
    140–44 (*see also* Branding)
  social currency of, 37, 39
  triggers and, 62, 66, 70, 79–85
  trustworthiness of stories versus,
    186
  virality of, 22, 196–98
  word of mouth versus, 8–10,
    43–44
  see also Public service announce-
    ments; *campaigns for specific
    products*
Airline frequent flier programs,
    44–45, 47–48
Alcohol abuse, 132–35, 139–40
Allport, Gordon, 199–200
Amazement, 22, 102, 188
Amazon.com, 8
American Airlines, 45
Anderson, Eric, 165
Anheuser-Busch, 86
Antista, Chris, 30
AOL, 140–41
Apple, 125–27, 142, 153
  "Think Different" campaign, 109
Arab Spring, 120
Archos, 142
Arend, Rene, 56
Arizona, University of, 132–33, 140
ARK Music Factory, 76
Armstrong, Lance, 144, 145
Arousal, 116–18
  physiological, 108–11
Atkins diet, 4
Autism, 99
  false information on connection
    of vaccines and, 176
Awards, 51
Awe, power of, 102–8

B

Baby names, 20
  popular, 5–6
Babywearing, 118–19

Balter, Dave, 62–63, 66
Barclay Prime (Philadelphia), 1–2, 170, 210
  hundred-dollar cheesesteak at, 2–4, 22, 23, 25, 42, 88–89, 196, 206, 207, 210
Barn raising, 159
Beauty, unrealistic standard of, 191–93
Beckham, David, 3
Behavioral residue, 24, 144–49, 153, 209
Bensimhon, Ron, 193–94, 199
Best Food Ever (television show), 3
Bhatia, Sabeer, 140–41
Binge drinking, 133–35, 139–40
Birds, The (movie), 203
Black, Rebecca, 75–77, 83, 92, 207
BlackBerry, 142
Blair Witch Project, 42–43
Blendtec, 16–18, 42, 43, 171, 208
  Will It Blend? campaign, 17–18, 22, 26*n,* 59, 182, 198, 206, 210
Blogs, 10, 26, 33
  emotions and, 95, 97, 119, 123
  public visibility of, 149
Bloomingdale's, 148
BMW, 103, 113
Bono, 224*n*
Book reviews, 8, 19, 80–81
Boring topics, *see* Interesting versus boring topics, word-of-mouth about
Boston Market, 84
Boyle, Susan, 103–105, 207
"Boy Who Cried Wolf, The," 183
Bradlow, Eric, 135
Branding, 210, 221*n*
  stories and, 193, 196, 198
  see also specific brands
Brigham Young University, 15, 16
Britain's Got Talent (television show), 103–104

Buckley, William F., Jr., 158
Budweiser beer, 79–80, 92
Bullying, campaigns against, 68
Burberry, 50–51, 142
Bush, George W., 75
Buzz, *see* Word of mouth
BzzAgent, 63–69, 78, 84, 221*n*

C
Cafaro, Anthony, 113–16, 123–24
Cambodian Americans, 205
Cancer:
  emotions evoked by, 103, 118
  promoting public awareness of, 137–38, 144–45, 153, 207
Carroll, Dave, 111–12
Cars:
  purchases of, 20, 36, 135, 217*n*
  repairs to, 186
Chanel, 143
Cheerios, 61–62, 66, 90–91, 206
Cheesesteak, hundred-dollar, 2–4, 22, 23, 25, 42, 88–89, 196, 206, 207, 210
Chicken McNuggets, 56
Chorak, Colleen, 81–82, 84, 92
Cialdini, Bob, 152
"Cinderella," 183
Clinton, Bill, 14
Clothing industry, 205
Coca-Cola, 70, 86, 113
College campuses, alcohol abuse on, 132–35, 139–40
Compaq, 142
Congress, U.S., 150
Consumer Reports, 36, 174
Contests, 50–51
Corn, shucking, 155–56
Corona beer, 61
Cosby, Bill, 14–15
Coupons, 64, 65
Craig, Ken, 155–56, 158, 206, 208

Creative, 142
Crest toothpaste, 7
Crick, Francis, 162–63
Crif Dogs, 29–31, 39
  bar at, *see* Please Don't Tell
CSI (television show), 122
Customer rewards, 52, 63, 170–71
  see also Frequent flier programs
Customer service, 43
  emotions evoked by, 109, 120
  remarkable, story about, 184–85,
    187, 189

D

Deal or No Deal (television show),
  122
Deals, psychology of, 162–70, 176
Delta Airlines Platinum Medallion,
  47–49
Democratic Party, 73
Diamond Multimedia, 142
Dickson, Tom, 15–18
Diet crazes, 4
Diminishing sensitivity, 166–68
DIRECTV, 42
Discounts, 51, 59, 206
  practical value of, 160–61, 164,
    166–71
Discover magazine, 94
Discovery channel, 3
Disney Corporation, 55, 99
  see also Walt Disney World
DNA, 163
Dole, Bob, 224*n*
Donut shops, 205
Dove products, 191–93, 206, 208
Drugs, 8
  effectiveness of, 5, 160
  performance-enhancing, 145
  recreational, campaign to
    discourage teens from
    using, 150–52
Dry cleaners, 205

E

eBay, 194
Einstein, Albert, 102, 162
Emmy Awards, 94
Emotions, evoking, 22, 23, 25,
    93–124, 205, 207–10
  of arousal, 108–12, 116–18
  of awe, 102–8
  exercise and, 120–23
  focus on, 112–16
  negative, 118–20
  practical value and 158, 160, 173,
    177
  in sharing, 96–101
  social currency and, 90
  through stories, 182, 188, 193, 201
Erectile dysfunction (ED), 149*n*
Evian, 196
Exclusivity, 31–33, 51–57, 59–60,
    169

F

Facebook, 7, 10, 12, 33, 40, 47, 57,
    149
False information, 5
  sharing, 176
  traction of, 120
Fantasy football, 57–58
Fast food, 20
  healthy, 188–89
  regional, 2
  see also McDonald's; Taco Bell
Fierce People (Wittenborn), 70
Fight-or-flight response, 108
Fischman, Ben, 51–53
Fitzsimons, Gráinne, 72
Flash sales, 52
Fogle, Jared, 188–89
Fortune 500 companies, 9
Foursquare, 48–49, 59
Free samples, 9, 64
Frequent flier programs, 44–45,
    47–48

G

Game mechanics, leveraging, 23, 36, 44–50, 59, 209
Gap, 35, 170
Gates, Bill, 14
GEICO, 79
Gilligan's Island (television show), 53
Giveaways, 148–49
Gladwell, Malcolm, 13
GoldenPalace.com, 194, 199
Google, 101, 119
  Creative Lab, 114–16
  "A Google a Day" trivia game, 114
  "Parisian Love" video, 113, 115–16, 123, 206
Gore, Al, 75
Grady, Denise, 93–97, 101, 103, 124
Grisham, John, 112
Grocery shopping, 50, 148, 174
  practical value in, 159, 168, 171
  reward programs for, 171
  stories about, 197–98
  triggers for, 71, 89–90
  word of mouth for, 68
Groupon, 160
Guerrilla marketing, 66
Guinness World Records, 196
Gurus, social media, 14, 62

H

Habitats, triggers in, 81–84, 92, 209
Haidt, Jonathan, 102
Halal Chicken and Gyro food cart (New York), 130–31
Halal Guys food cart (New York), 131
Hargreaves, David, 71
Harvard University, 33, 46–47
Healthy habits, promoting, 4, 8, 10, 95
  emotions versus information in, 112–13, 118

stories for, 187–89
  triggers for, 71–73, 87–89
Heath, Chip and Dan, 21, 101
Hedren, Tippi, 203–6
Herd mentality, *see* Social proof
Hershey candy company, 81–82
Hire, The (short film series), 117
Hitchcock, Alfred, 203
Holiday Inn Express, 65
Holly, Buddy, 197
Homer, 180
Honda, 113
Hope Village, 203
Hornik, Bob, 150–52
Hotmail, 140–41, 153, 206
Hot Topic, 35

I

iCraze, 125
Illinois, University of, 40
iMac, 125
Imitation, 23, 127–32, 134, 153
Immediate word of mouth, 67–69, 78
Immigrants, niche businesses of, 203–6
Infomercials, 164–65
Insiders, feeling like, *see* Exclusivity; Scarcity
Intel, 153
Interesting versus boring topics, word-of-mouth about, 15, 100–1
  social currency of, 39–42
  triggers for, 62, 66–69, 78–79, 90
International Babywearing Week, 118
Internet, 84, 117, 127, 140–41, 156, 181
  casinos on, 168
  see also specific servers and websites
iPhone, 110, 123, 174
iPod, 142–43, 206

Irish Americans, 205
Iyengar, Raghu, 34

J
Jack Link's, 40
JetBlue, 42
Jewish immigrants, 205
Jobs, Steve, 125–27
Johannessen, Koreen, 132–33, 140
Jokes, 14, 36, 38, 105, 110
"Just Say No" anti-drug campaign,
    150–51

K
Kahneman, Daniel, 162, 163
Keller Fay Group, 11
Keltner, Dacher, 102
Kidney donations, 129–30
Kit Kat, 81–85, 92, 208
Korean Americans, 205

L
L.L. Bean, 165
Lacoste, 142
Lamborghinis, 58–59
Lance Armstrong Foundation,
    145–46
  see also Livestrong
Land's End, 165, 184–85, 187, 189
Late Show, 3
Lauren, Ralph, 65, 124
Le, Thuan, 203–5
Letterman, David, 3
LGBT community, 149*n*
Liquor stores, 205
Livestrong, 4, 206
  wristbands, 144–47, 153, 229–30*n*
LivingSocial, 160
Logos, 126–27, 142, 153
Louboutin, Christian, 143
Loyalty marketing, *see* Customer
    rewards
Lululemon, 148, 153

M
MacEachern, Scott, 144–47
Made to Stick (Heath), 21, 116
Mad Men (television show), 62
"Man Drinks Fat" (public service
    announcement), 87–88, 118,
    206
March of Dimes, 65
Marlboro cigarettes, 83–85
Mars, Franklin, 71
Mars candy company, 70–71, 83
Massachusetts Institute of
    Technology (MIT), 130
McDonald's, 56–57
McKendrick, Jennifer, 71
McNeil Consumer Healthcare, 118
McShane, Blake, 135
Medicines, *see* Drugs
Meehan, Jim, 32, 55*n*
Meredith, Marc, 74
Michelob beer, 86
Microsoft, 143
Milkman, Katherine, 99
Millikan, Robert, 94
Miracle Blade knives, 164, 165
Mitchell, Jason, 33
MoneyWhys, 173, 208
Mormons, 15–16
Most E-Mailed lists, 40, 93–94,
    96–98, 103, 105, 107–8, 173
  emotions and, 108, 113
  systematic analysis of, 98–101
  public visibility and, 145
Motivation, 29, 45–46, 57–59, 77
Motrin, 118–20
Moustaches, public visibility of,
    136–39, 153, 207
Movember Foundation, 138–39,
    153, 206
Movies, 42, 164
  emotions evoked by, 108, 117
  reviews of, 7
  social currency of, 40, 43, 55

Movies (*cont.*)
  word of mouth about, 13, 15, 68, 221*n*
Music, 75–76
  digital players, 142–43
  emotions and, 102, 112, 115
  illegal downloads of, 152
  public visibility and, 149
  social currency of, 35–36
  stories and, 180
Muzak, 71

N
Nail salons, 203–5
Narratives, *see* Stories
National Aeronautic and Space Administration (NASA), 70–71
National Youth Anti-Drug Media Campaign, 150
New England Journal of Medicine, The, 83
New York City Department of Health (DOH), 87–88
New York magazine, 130
New York Times, The, 20, 94–96, 102, 119
  book review, 80–81
  Most E-mailed list, 40, 93, 97–101, 103–5, 107, 174, 224*n*
NeXT Computer, 125
Niche businesses, immigrant-owned, 203–5
Nike, 142, 144–46
Baller Bands, 145
Nobel Prize, 162–63
Nonprofits, 10, 25*n*, 26, 113, 206
  see also specific organizations and foundations
North, Adrian, 71
Novelty, 39, 42, 66–67

O
Obama, Barack, 103

Obesity, campaigns against, *see* Healthy habits, promoting
Observability, *see* Public visibility
Odyssey, The (Homer), 157
O'Hare Airport, 111
Olympics, 50, 118, 193–95, 199
Ongoing word of mouth, 67–69, 78
Opinion leaders, 13
Organ transplants, 129–30

P
PageRank algorithms, 113
Panda cheese, 197–98
Pathfinder mission, 70–71
Pay it forward, prosocial ideal of, 159
Pennebaker, Jamie, 93
Pennsylvania, University of, 17
Petrified Forest National Park, 152–53
Philips, 63
Photoshop, 190–91
Physics Today magazine, 94
Physiological arousal, 108–12
Pinocchio (movie), 55
Piper, Tim, 189–92
Please Don't Tell, 31–32, 39, 54, 55*n*, 59–60, 169, 206
Politics, 20, 26, 131, 158
  emotions evoked by, 120, 123
  practical value in, 160
  triggers and, 75
  word of mouth in, 10, 13
  see also Voting behavior
Polling places, influence on voter behavior of, 73–75
Postman, Joseph, 199–200
PowerBook G4, 110
Practical value, 24, 25, 26*n*, 94, 155–77, 205, 207–10
  of information, 101, 172–76
  public visibility and, 141
  remarkable, 168–72

of saving money, 160–68
of stories, 182, 188
Price, 5–7, 16, 57, 186
  high, *see* Cheesesteak,
    hundred-dollar
  public visibility and, 146
  practical value and, 160–71
  social currency and, 51–56
  of stocks, impact of emotion
    on, 112
Pringles, 143
Private sales, 52
Product reviews, 20, 182
Promotional offers, 63
  practical value of, 160, 168–71
  see also Discounts
Prospect theory, 163–68
Prostate Cancer Foundation of
  Australia, 138
Public service announcements
  (PSAs), 86–90, 112–13, 118,
  149–52
Public visibility, 20, 23–25, 26*n*,
  125–53, 205, 207, 209
  antithetical effects of, 149–53
  behavioral residue and,
    144–49
  emotions evoked by, 97, 115
  imitation and, 127–32
  power of, 132–36
  practical value and, 172
  providing private concerns
    with, 136–40
  through self-advertising,
    140–44
  social currency and, 54
  stories and, 192, 201

Q

Quality, 5–7, 25, 196, 210
  of buzz, 59, 130
  low, 56
  see also Practical Value

R

Rasmussen, Scott, 80
Reagan, Nancy, 150
Reduced prices, *see* Discounts
Reese's Pieces, 89
Reference price, 165
Remarkability, 22, 26*n,* 31–32,
  36–44, 59
  of practical value, 168–72
  public visibility and, 141
  of stories, 185, 188, 194–95
  triggers and, 69, 89
Republican Party, 73
Restaurants, 36, 38, 40, 48, 174–75
  casual dining, *see* Boston Market;
    Crif Dogs
  high-end, *see* Barclay Prime
  practical value of, 170, 177
  public visibility of, 127–28, 148
  reviews of, 127, 174, 175
  triggers for, 84
  word of mouth for, 2–3, 10, 22,
    23, 53, 64, 66
Reusable bags, 89–90, 148
Reviews, 149
  book, 8, 19, 80–81
  movie, 7
  product, 20, 182
  restaurant, 127, 174, 175
Rolex watches, 54
"Roller Babies" video, 196
Rubenstein, Marke, 37–38
Rue La La, 52–54, 55*n,* 59, 169, 206
Rumors, 13, 26, 199
  false, emotions evoked by, 120
  on social media, 7

S

Sales, 5, 10
  emotions and, 117
  negative publicity and, 20, 80–81
  practical value and, 161, 164–66,
    169

Sales (cont.)
  public visibility and, 135, 142
  social currency and, 51–53, 56,
      210
  stories and, 192, 196
  triggers for, 20, 63–64, 70–71,
      80–83
  word of mouth and, 8, 18
Sample sales, 52
Scarcity, 54–57, 59, 169
School of Visual Arts, 113
Schwartz, Eric, 66
Secrecy, see Exclusivity
Segall, Ken, 125, 127
Shakespeare, William, 183
Shake Weight, 81
Sharing:
  emotions and, 96–101
  self-, 36, 59
  see also Word of mouth
Shebairo, Brian, 30–31
Silk nondairy milk products, 65
Simester, Duncan, 165
Six Sigma management
      strategy, 4
SmartBargains.com, 51–52
  Smart Shopper loyalty club, 52
Smith, Jack, 140–41
Smoking cessation, see Healthy
      habits, promoting
Snapple, 37–39
Snow White (movie), 55
Social currency, 22–23, 25, 26n,
      29–60, 205, 207–10
  emotions and, 101, 103, 106
  of exclusivity and scarcity, 31–33,
      51–57, 59–60
  of inner remarkability, 37–44
  leveraging game mechanics for,
      44–51
  motivation and, 57–59
  practical value and, 158–60,
      168–70, 177

public visibility and, 139, 141–42,
      147–48
  of self-sharing, 33–36
  stories and, 181, 188, 201
  triggers and, 62, 66, 69, 77, 90
Social epidemics, 4, 13, 18, 206–7
Social media, 10–12, 62, 119–20
  see also Facebook; Twitter;
      YouTube
Social proof, 128–31, 134, 141–44,
      147, 148, 151, 153
Social transmission, 7–10, 26–27
  see also Social media; Word of
      mouth
Solitaire, 46
Sonicare electric toothbrushes,
      63–64
Sons of Maxwell, 111
Sorensen, Alan, 80
South Beach diet, 4
Spiegel, 165
Spotify, 149
Stapleton, Bill, 146
Starwood Hotels, 1
Status symbols, 23
  airline rewards programs as,
      44–45, 47–49
  credit cards as, 49–50
  public visibility of, 148
  scarcity and exclusivity of, 55
STEPPS, 25, 207–10
  see also Emotions, evoking; Social
      Currency; Practical Value;
      Public visibility; Stories;
      Triggers
Stockholm University, 162
Stories, 7, 13, 21–22, 24–26,
      179–201, 203–5, 207
  emotions evoked by, 106–7, 121
  learning through, 186–89
  practical value of, 158, 172, 175,
      210
  social currency of, 39–42

Trojan horse, 189–93, 209
as vessels, 181–86
virality of, 193–201
Subway sandwich chain, 187–89
Sudoku puzzles, 46
Sunny Delight, 71
Super Bowl, 224*n*
Supermarkets, *see* Grocery
shopping
Surprise, generating, 67, 102
by breaking expected patterns, 42
in stories, 22, 188

T
Taco Bell, 64
Tamir, Diana, 33
Targeting, 8–10, 72, 79
Terra Blues, 42
Thaler, Richard, 163
Thelonious Monk Institute of
Jazz, 112
Tide detergent, 7
Tiffany, 148
Time magazine, 94, 112
Tipping Point, The (Gladwell), 13,
19, 21
Tour de France, 144, 146
Triggers, 23, 25, 61–92, 205,
207–10
affected on behavior of, 69–75
context of, 77–81
days of week as, 75–77
effective, frequency of stimulus
for, 85–90
emotions evoked by, 95, 118
habitat for, 81–85
immediate versus ongoing, 67–69
practical value and, 158, 177
public visibility of, 136
stories as, 186, 189, 201
Trojan Horse, 24, 179–82, 191, 199,
200
Truth, 5, 176

Tversky, Amos, 163
Twitter, 10, 12–13, 47, 48, 57, 90,
119, 208
Tylenol, 40

U
United Airlines, 111–12
Premier status, 44–45, 47
Urban legends, 20, 183
USA Today, 3
U2, 224*n*

V
Vacuum cleaners, 157–58
Vanguard, 173–74, 177, 208
Viagra, 149*n*
Victoria's Secret, 148
Videos, 40, 97, 114–15, 191–92,
196, 208, 210
emotional response to, 103–5,
114–15, 123–24
public service announcement,
87–88, 149–51
see also YouTube; *titles of specific
videos*
Vietnamese refugees, 203–6
Village People, 81
Village Squire Restaurants, 40
Virality, 6–7*n,* 13–15, 17–18, 20,
22, 201, 208, 209
emotion and, 93–100, 103–12,
115, 120
practical value and, 155–58,
174–75,
social currency and, 26, 32
stories and, 24, 193–201
triggers and, 66, 76–77
Virgil, 180
Voting behavior, 128, 207
public visibility and, 147–48,
153
triggers and, 73–75
word of mouth and, 7, 13, 51, 68

W

Walkman, 143

Wall Street Journal, The, 3, 98–99

Walt Disney World, 61–62, 66, 90, 158

Watson, James D., 162–63

Watts, Duncan, 206

Weber grills, 161

Websites, 5, 7, 32, 38, 81, 97, 131
  content, 97–98, 123
  game mechanics and, 48, 50–51
  practical value of, 160, 174, 177
  public visibility and, 136, 139, 144, 149, 152
  word of mouth about, 216*n*
  see also specific websites

Wein, Howard, 1–2, 210

Wells Fargo, 39–40

Wharton School, 17, 18, 34, 105, 136–37, 148

Wheeler, Christian, 74

Word of mouth, 7–15, 20, 21–22, 27, 208–10
  emotions and, 117, 122
  game mechanics and, 48

generating, 10–15, 39, 55, 59
  (*see also* BzzAgent)
immediate versus ongoing, 67–69, 78
online, 11–12, 39 (*see also* Most E-mailed lists)
in political campaigns, 51
products and services worthy of, 15–18
public visibility and, 136, 141
stories and, 181, 194–96
triggers for, 62, 67, 77–81, 84, 90–91, 205
see also Social currency

Wright, George, 16, 206

Y

"YMCA" (song), 81

YouTube, 6–7, 10, 12, 17, 20, 67, 110, 112, 123, 156

Z

Zhang, Juanjuan, 130

Ziploc bags, 78–79